P9-CFX-029

ACQUISITION OF READING

Cognitive, Linguistic, and Perceptual Prerequisites

Edited by **Frank B. Murray, Ph.D.**, H. Rodney Sharp Professor of Educational Psychology; and **John J. Pikulski, Ph.D.**, Associate Professor of Education, both at The University of Delaware

This book thoroughly analyzes cognitive, linguistic, and perceptual prerequisites for the acquisition of reading and critically reviews current research on these prerequisites. No other current text offers such thorough coverage of the problem of reading acquisition in the areas of intellectual development, learning, perception, linguistics, and information processing.

Five major chapters cover the main prerequisite areas. Each chapter is followed by a critique or response that presents alternate viewpoints and further illuminates the study of reading prerequisites. The underlying assumption throughout is that intelligent instruction in reading should be based upon the child's prior and relevant acquisitions in perception, cognition, intellect, language, and learning.

The book includes an analysis of the implications of Piaget's theory for reading and focuses on the nature of prerequisites as they develop in pre-school children, while also covering the acquisition of literacy by adults.

The Acquisition of Reading is the definitive class text for courses on the psychology of reading and valuable collateral reading for studies in educational psychology, reading, and cognitive psychology. It is also a stimulating professional text and reference source for psychologists and educators interested in the reading process and an essential acquisition for libraries serving departments of education and psychology.

THE ACQUISITION OF READING

Cognitive, Linguistic, and Perceptual Prerequisites

edited by

Frank B. Murray, Ph. D.,
H. Rodney Sharp Professor,
University of Delaware

and

John J. Pikulski, Ph. D.,
Associate Professor,
University of Delaware

University Park Press
Baltimore

UNIVERSITY PARK PRESS
International Publishers in Science and Medicine
233 East Redwood Street
Baltimore, Maryland 21202

Copyright © 1978 by University Park Press

Typeset by Everybodys Press
Manufactured in the United States of America
by the Maple Press Company

Taken from the proceedings of the Second Delaware Symposium on
Curriculum, Learning, and Instruction, Newark, Del., 1975.

Library of Congress Cataloging in Publication Data

Delaware Symposium on Curriculum, Learning, and Instruction, 2d,
   Newark, Del., 1975.
    The acquisition of reading: cognitive, linguistic, and perceptual
prerequisites.

    1. Reading—Congresses. I. Murray, Frank B. II. Pikulski, John J.
III. Title.
LB1049.95.D44   1975   428'.4   78-7390
ISBN 0-8391-1281-5

Contents

Contributors

Sylvia Farnham-Diggory, Ph.D., Dept. of Educational Foundations, University of Delaware, Newark, DE   19711

Hans Furth, Ph.D., Dept. of Psychology, Catholic University of America, Washington, DC   20017

Roberta Golinkoff, Ph.D., Dept. of Educational Foundations, University of Delaware, Newark, DE   19711

John Guthrie, Ph.D., International Reading Association, 800 Barksdale Road, Newark, DE   19711

Ludwig Mosberg, Ph.D., Dept. of Educational Foundations, University of Delaware, Newark, DE   19711

Frank B. Murray, Ph.D., Dept. of Educational Foundations, University of Delaware, Newark, DE 19711

Anne Pick, Ph.D., Institute of Child Development, University of Minnesota, Minneapolis, MN   55455

John J. Pikulski, Ph.D., Dept. of Educational Foundations, University of Delaware, Newark, DE 19711

Thomas Sticht, Ph.D., National Institute of Education, 1200 19th Street, N.W., Washington, DC   20208

Richard Venezky, Ph.D., Dept. of Educational Foundations, University of Delaware, Newark, DE   19711

Introduction

Frank B. Murray

By itself, the fact that reading rarely appears spontaneously or as a result of instruction before an age of four years or so prompts a search for prerequisite conditions for its development. Because the four-year-old child shows considerable linguistic, perceptual, and cognitive competence, it seems reasonable to investigate the degree to which accomplishments in perception, language, and cognition provide necessary and sufficient conditions for the emergence of reading.

If from the beginning of the child's life the primary medium of social communication were writing and reading instead of speaking and listening, and if from the beginning the child were submerged in a bath of print instead of speech and was forced to communicate solely through writing and reading, we might find that reading would develop as naturally as we find language and speech developing in children. As it is, the child is a speaker before he is a reader, and his reading is commonly dependent upon systematic instruction rather than the other way around. Were it not for the fact that the various instructional strategies lead to uneven success in reading achievement and that reading skill is difficult for many children to acquire, reading would not in all probability have attracted the attention it has from researchers in education and psychology.

These prerequisites for reading were the subjects of the Second Delaware Symposium on Curriculum, Learning, and Instruction that was held at the University of Delaware in June 1975. The underlying assumption was that intelligent instruction in initial reading should be based upon the child's prior and relevant acquisitions in perception, cognition, intellect, language, and learning. The members of the symposium panel were Sylvia Farnham-Diggory, Hans Furth, Roberta Golinkoff, John Guthrie, Ludwig Mosberg, Frank Murray, Anne Pick, John Pikulski, Thomas Sticht, and Richard Venezky. Professors Farnham-Diggory, Furth, Pick, Sticht, and Venezky presented formal papers that were critiqued formally by one other member of the panel, followed by open discussion by the audience and panel. The chapters in this book are substantially updated revisions of those presentations.

To some extent Richard Venezky, then of the University of Wisconsin, challenged the symposium assumption that reading instruction should be based upon prereading skills. In his paper, the first of the meeting, he critically and quickly reviewed the literature on common reading methods, grapheme/phoneme correspondences, the management and organization of the schools, and basic psychological research on prereading competence and concluded that although much remains unknown about these areas, researchers in reading should focus upon visual word recognition. This is the heart of reading skill. Although the recognition of words is constrained by many factors, Venezky thought the most promising approach to understanding how we recognize words is to evaluate the influence of orthographic structure in word recognition. His position provoked criticism by Golinkoff and other members of the panel and audience who argued that other linguistic features, such as phonemic segmentation or linguistic awareness, provided more promising approaches to understanding the reading process.

Hans Furth further provided controversy by claiming not that reading was essentially word recognition, but that instruction in reading might not even be necessary if the child was challenged by a program of experience that promoted the development of the thinking operations described by Piaget. On theoretical grounds he argued that the acquisition of reading does not contribute to the development of intelligence as viewed from the Piagetian perspective. This claim was challenged by Murray and several members of the panel and audience.

The contribution of information processing prerequisites for reading was turned by Sylvia Farnham-Diggory into a heuristic for research on reading. Somewhat facetiously she described the developmental stages in psychology's interest in reading phenomena. Computer simulation models of reading, one of which she described, are at least attempts to describe what could be going on in the child's head when he begins to read. To date, the main contribution of the approach is that it has at least asked the right question, that is, what goes on in our heads when we learn to read.

This general line of argument was continued by Anne Pick, who argued that the research on the perceptual components of reading suffers from lack of a conceptual analysis of the reading task that has ecological validity. She described a number of perceptual models of reading that provided a rationale for her own research in the perceptual requirements in reading a word. The results of research on reading were also instructive for the field of perceptual development.

The final paper, by Thomas Sticht, raised the interesting question of initial reading acquisition by adults and examined the all-important relationship between a person's competence with spoken and with written language. Although it is obvious that language is fairly well developed before reading begins, the dependence of reading upon speech comprehension and production is often alleged and by no means obvious. Sticht argued that learning to read is part of a general set of learning skills that has no unique relationship to prior language acquisition.

There was consensus that development of sound instructional strategies for teaching initial reading would be facilitated by the development of conceptual models that simulated the mental mechanisms required in tasks that had ecological validity as reading tasks. At the very least this required a formal and precise examination of what is required of a mind that can recognize words.

This symposium limited its discussion to the transition from non-reading to reading, the heart of which was acknowledged to be the ability to recognize words, to pronounce them, or to decode them. It remains for another symposium group to ponder not simply what it means to read, but what it means to read well.

In closing the symposium, Murray noted that within the last fifty years good penmanship, the skill of forming legible and sometimes elegant marks, has nearly disappeared as an instructional goal and valued skill in contemporary society. At the turn of the century the possession of a good hand was a criterion for employment and a sign of gentility. With the advent of the hand electronic calculator, arithematical skills that so preoccupy the elementary school child may soon become as little valued as a knowledge of Latin is for most people today. As it becomes more possible to function profitably in an electronic media society without any appreciable need for acquiring information by a sustained reading effort, the reading skill could become as quaint and as insignificant a skill as fine penmanship is in contemporary society. Nevertheless, the skills needed to access language in a nonreading society presumably will depend upon the development of competencies similar to the prereading competencies. We suppose these competencies would be generated and enhanced by the very same scientific study described in the following chapters.

THE
ACQUISITION
OF READING

READING ACQUISITION:
The Occult and the Obscure
Richard L. Venezky

INTRODUCTION

The accouterments of reading—especially the alphabet—have long been objects of mystery and misunderstanding. Socrates, who was usually quite sober and objective, claimed that the alphabet was invented by the Egyptian god Thoth but rejected by the reigning king of Egypt, out of fear that writing would impair man's memory and that people would read without understanding—a prophecy that perhaps has not been totally unrealized.

The earliest Germanic invaders of Briton brought with them an alphabet that was restricted to mystical applications. The term applied to the letters of this alphabet, *rune,* itself originated from the Old English word for *mystery.* At about the same time that Briton was being invaded by rune-carrying Germanics, St. Augustine was observing St. Ambrose read without moving his lips—an act that was, in Augustine's words, both surprising and perplexing.

The acquisition of reading has had no less a connection with the occult and obscure. The Greeks and Romans held that men of high rank who had lived evil lives would be forced to maintain themselves in the next world by teaching reading and writing. In the United States as in England, the teaching of religion and reading were united for several hundred years. The Hornbook and the New England primers, the earliest American reading systems, devoted more space to religious themes than to the basics of reading.

In literature, the mysteries of reading acquisition have also been perpetuated. Tarzan, as probably few remember, taught himself to read English at a time when his communicative repertoire was limited to basic Snake, Monkey, and Elephant. This was possible, his creator tells us, because of the "active intelligence of a healthy mind endowed by inheritance with more than

1

ordinary reasoning powers" (Burroughs, 1912:24). (No doubts are expressed here about the relative potencies of nature and nurture.) Shakespeare presented a similar view in *Much Ado About Nothing:* "To be a well-favored man is the gift of fortune, but to write and read comes by nature."

Mayakovsky, the controversial poet of the Russian revolution, also laid claim to self-taught literacy:

> The human fledgling—
> barely out of the egg—
> grasps at a book,
> and quires of exercise paper.
> But I learned my alphabet
>   from signboards,
> leafing through pages of iron
>   and tin.
>
> (Vladimir Mayakovsky, "My University")

The case for the occult in present-day reading may not be overwhelming, even with divination in the guise of predictive tests and attempts to find truth from the dead, as revealed in the recent obsession with Huey and Cattell, but the case for the obscure is undeniable. That most educators view reading acquisition as an obscure process is evident from the willingness with which they adopt and defend unfounded solutions to reading problems. If one judged the current status of the knowledge of reading acquisition by the amount of agreement found among schools on any instructional practice, then the conclusion would have to be that reading acquisition remains completely enveloped in darkness.

The situation found among researchers is not wholly different. Some attribute reading problems to dialect differences, others to the irregularities of English orthography, and still others to cross-modal integration problems. These are but a few of the postulated sources of reading failure, but they are sufficient to show that after almost a century of research many people hold that the acquisition of literacy is an obscure process at best. The result of this unwarranted belief is not only unconscionable practices in the classrooms but wasted efforts in research.

Whatever the uncertainties in our knowledge of reading acquisition, there are clearly some results from the last century of research that have a bearing on instruction and on the direction that research should or should not take. However limited these results may be, there is still some merit in sorting out the various trends that are evidenced today in reading research in the hope that such an activity will lead to identification of major issues in reading acquisition. The purpose of this chapter is to suggest areas of research and development that have the greatest potential for furthering the teaching of reading.

Because the ultimate concern here is the improvement of reading instruction, research topics that, although important for gaining a basic understanding of reading acquisition, deal with skills that all children appear to acquire without difficulty will not be discussed. Also ignored are problems related to cultural, language, and dialect differences, and to handicaps. It is important, however, to clarify from the outset that some of the conclusions drawn will be without strong experimental support and some will be outright speculation. Given the paucity of data in some areas of reading, there is little choice in an integrative summary such as this but to select the most logical path and assume along with Francis Bacon that "truth will emerge more rapidly from error than from chaos."

THE APPLIED RESEARCH TREND

Two major trends in research on reading acquisition have co-existed since at least the turn of the century: the applied and the theoretical. Both are concerned ultimately with improving reading instruction and both claim to originate from experimentally derived information. But beyond these similarities the two are no more closely related than lightning is to the lightning bug.

The applied trend is concerned with instructional methods. It is behavioristic and often pragmatic; it begins with a proposed solution, and then searches backwards for a justification. In this last characteristic—and in several others—the products of this trend resemble those of religions. New methods are often launched by individuals who possess, at least for some, an irresistable charisma. These persons have become privy to revealed truth in the form of a new teaching method, and proselytize in its name. As their following enlarges, they attempt to anchor the new method in some form of legitimate research just as religions search out previous writings in an attempt to prove that they are the true continuation of the original church. It should be no surprise, therefore, that among those who have been responsible for widely used teaching methods in the past century are a Civil War colonel, a doctor, a public relations specialist, and a printer.

Methods

The most conspicuous concerns of this trend are the so-called methods of teaching reading: phonics, linguistics, whole word, and the like. There are probably no curricular concerns over which more ink has been unnecessarily spilled or more chaos perpetuated than these. Legions of reading specialists and misled graduate students, egged on by reputable educators, have compared Method A to Method B ad infinitum and ad nauseum. Only a few points need to be emphasized in summarizing the research on these methods. First, none of the popularized methods is sufficiently well defined to be testable. Each is concerned primarily with the earliest stages of reading instruction—often only the first year or less—with nearly total disregard for comprehension. Most decisions that classroom teachers must make on grouping, diagnosis, rate of presentation, use of exemplars, type of learning, reinforcement, review, and the like cannot be made on the basis of the definitions of any of these methods.

Second, most methods regardless of their titles depend heavily on letter-sound learning, the basic difference among them occurring in the timing of such instruction. The phonics/linguistics group tends to start out with heavier doses of letters and sounds than the whole-word group, and the language-experience school is usually vague on this point. For these reasons, no further concern will be given here to the traditionally defined reading methods. Although publishers will continue to extoll the virtues of phonics or whatever method, there is every reason to believe that only a small part of the variance in reading acquisition is attributable to the real effects of such ill-defined practices. Some support has been given to this conclusion by the Cooperative First Grade Reading Study (Bond and Dykstra, 1967). However, more important corroboration can be found in recent studies of school factors and reading achievement, which will be described shortly.

Orthography

Intentionally omitted from the discussion above was research on reformed orthographies such as the Initial Teaching Alphabet (ITA). These approaches to reading instruction are based on the premise that the major block to successful acquisition of literacy is the irregularity of English orthography. Sir James Pitman, the chief advocate in England of the ITA, claims "Even if taught entirely by look-and-say, the child will nevertheless, at his own time, begin to discern and take advantage of the alphabetic nature of the material, and so extend his reading vocabulary to the full potential. The wonder is that any child should learn by a phonic approach since T.O. [Traditional Orthography] is as unsuitable for phonic as it is for look-and-say" (Pitman, 1961:10). This opinion has also been advanced by a number of distinguished linguists. Bloomfield, for example, held that "the difficulty of our spelling greatly delays elementary education, and wastes even much time of adults. When one sees the admirably consistent orthographies of Spanish, Bohemian, and Finnish, one naturally wishes that a similar system might be adopted for English" (Bloomfield, 1933:500−502).

Yet there are no experimental or observational data to justify this claim and a considerable amount to negate it. The most often cited evidence in favor of reformed orthography is the supposedly low failure rate in initial reading acquisition in Finland and Japan, countries whose languages have highly consistent letter-sound relationships. Downing (1973), for example, makes this claim and concludes from it that children in English-speaking countries will learn to read faster with a regularized spelling for English. This argument is inconsistent in its logic and factually questionable. In neither Finland no Japan do we find cultures or educational systems that are in any way comparable to either England or the United States. In Finland, for example, children enter their first year of reading instruction at the age of 7, in contrast to 6 in the United States and 5 in England. In addition, Finland has an extremely homogeneous population, with over 90% of its population speaking the same language and belonging to the same religion. Due to these factors, plus an extensive social welfare system, Finland has no sizable underprivileged groups or disenfranchised minorities—the very groups in the United States that show the highest failure rate in initial reading instruction.

More importantly, there are orthographies that approach the consistency of Finnish and Japanese, such as Spanish and Rumanian, but for which extensive reading failure has been evidenced. If orthographic regularity were a primary determinant of reading success, we would expect a gradation of reading failure among educationally advanced countries, based on characteristics of the orthography in use, but no such gradation has ever been established.

There is also direct evidence that tends to negate the reformed orthography argument. In several studies on letter-sound learning, the degree of regularity in a letter-sound correspondence pattern was not found to be a good predictor of how well that pattern was learned (Venezky, Chapman, and Calfee, 1972; Venezky, 1974). For example, the long and short vowel patterns (final e vs. final consonant) were learned to a considerably higher degree than the initial c patterns,[1] even though the latter are simpler and more consistent than the former. This finding was replicated by Venezky and Johnson (1973), and seems to result from the number of exemplars that are introduced for each pattern.

Finally, it should be noted that the reformed orthography advocates seldom attend to instructional questions beyond the introduction of their proposed alphabets. Would it be acceptable, for example, to introduce ITA in conjunction with a whole-word approach?

In summary, there is little support and some counterevidence for the reformed orthography approach to reading instruction. This is not to say that some teachers won't be successful in using ITA, Unifon, or any other reformed system. There is no reason to doubt the numerous claims of success that have been made for these systems, or in fact for any method. But as a major approach either to improving reading instruction on a large scale or to gaining a better understanding of how children learn to read, reformed spelling holds little promise.

Management

A third applied research area centers not on the specific teaching method or spelling system used, but on the manner in which the total reading program is managed within a school building.

---

[1] That is, the patterns in which initial c appears before e, i, or y (and is therefore soft), or before any other letter (and is therefore hard).

On one level of concern are the skill management systems, such as the Wisconsin Design for Reading Skill Development (Quilling and Otto, 1971). These systems are based on the specifications of testable subskills that are arranged in either a linear sequence or a hierarchy. The management system defines the skills, specifies assessment procedures for each (usually criterion-referenced tests), and provides record-keeping mechanisms and a resource file that relates skills to instructional components in one or more commercially available programs. Such management systems can be criticized on a variety of grounds, such as the skills that are selected, the skill sequencing, and the overemphasis on testing. However, they do encourage teachers to attend to individual needs. Research in this area has been limited so far to establishing relationships among subskills, and has yet to show much promise for improving the teaching of reading. What remains to be pursued, however, is the impact of these systems on teacher behavior.

On a different level are attempts to totally restructure the school organization so that individual needs can be better served and teachers can work more efficiently. One such system, called the multi-unit school (which is a component of Individually Guided Education [Klausmeier, Rossmiller, and Saily, 1977]), groups classes into units and assigns differential roles to teachers. Typically, kindergarten, first, and second grades form one unit and third, fourth, and fifth grades form another. Each unit has a unit leader plus teachers and aides. The unit leaders within a school direct their unit staffs and also serve as a curricular planning board. For reading instruction, the unit team decides how children will be grouped and what work they will do. What is most encouraging about such schemes is that they stress the total educational system within a school, rather than a single component of it. However, too few evaluative data are available to objectively assess the success of such efforts.

But perhaps more important for reading success than skill management or school organizational models is the total management of the reading program within the school structure. This has been emphasized in two recent studies of schools that succeeded in teaching reading to disadvantaged students (Weber, 1971; State of New York, 1974). In the Weber study, the successful schools were characterized by (among other features): strong, well-identified leadership; careful diagnosis of individual abilities; and continuing education for teachers. The 1974 State of New York study concluded that "the differences in pupils' reading achievement [in the schools studied] were primarily attributable to administrative policies, behavior, procedures and practices" (p. 20). Leadership in instruction in reading (principal, assistant principal, or group of dedicated teachers) was also noted as a significant variable. Even though the methodologies of these studies require careful scrutiny, the results provide compelling motivation for further use of the subjective, case analysis approach.[2]

The process of reading instruction, including staff development, resource allocation, attitudes, and leadership, needs careful scrutiny. Other than studies of student-teacher or student-student interaction (e.g., Flanders, 1970), few accounts are available on how reading instruction is planned and carried out within a school and classroom. The two studies described above are a step towards the procurement of such information.

Educators have tended for too long to blame the reading instruction when children fail to learn to read, whereas in many—if not most—situations the school system as a whole is at fault. Whatever we may learn about the reading process or about the development of reading ability, overcrowded schools with untrained and disinterested teachers will seldom achieve a high degree of success in teaching reading. The sooner we understand what is crucial to successful instruction, the sooner we can reallocate increasingly limited resources in an optimal way.

THE THEORY-BASED RESEARCH TREND

The second trend in studies of reading acquisition could loosely be termed *theory-based research*. It is pursued more out of concern for general psychological problems than for improving the teaching of reading per se. The earliest experimental studies in this trend, those of Cattell, Dodge, Erdmann, Quantz, and others, were motivated by an interest in the speed of mental events. Reading was a conveniently observable behavior whose component processes appeared amenable to precise measurement. Similarly, in the late 1950s when research on reading was revived by experimental psychologists, the primary areas of study

---

[2] For a review of these and other school factor studies, see Venezky, 1978.

were those of general psychological concern, such as the development of perceptual abilities.[3]

For theory-based studies on reading, the task of identifying productive avenues to pursue is quite difficult. Reading research is extremely broad, encompassing disciplines as diverse as psychology, neurology, opthalmology, typography, and education. Rather than attempting to be comprehensive, the discussion here is limited to the linguistic and cognitive aspects of the preparation of children for formal reading instruction (often called reading readiness) and the development of basic reading skills at the primary level. These are complementary research concerns that differ considerably in the types of theory that they draw upon and the experimental paradigms that they employ.

Preparation for Reading

Research on the prereading child has concentrated recently on three main areas: 1) understanding of the reading task; 2) language development; and 3) perceptual and cognitive skills.

Understanding of the Reading Task   There can be no doubt that some children enter reading instruction with a well-formed concept of what reading is all about; they recognize many of the letters by name, know a few words by sight, and may attempt to sound out sentences. These children will learn to read under almost any teaching method, even one centered upon the local telephone directory. But many children do not enter the reading situation so well prepared. More often than not they are unaware of either the purpose or the nature of reading; they do not know that letters represent sounds, and that these sounds can be blended into words and words into meaningful sentences. Some researchers associate this lack of understanding with reading failure. For example, Reid (1966), who interviewed children during their first year of reading instruction in Scotland, writes that ". . . reading, prior to the experience, is a mysterious activity to which they [the children] come with only the vaguest of expectancies. In some cases the children. . . were not even clear whether one 'read' the pictures or the other 'marks' on the paper" (p. 60).

Similar studies in the United States and in Canada have shown that, under certain experimental conditions, children are

---

[3] See Venezky, 1977, for a history of research on reading processes.

not sure of the difference between sounds and words prior to and often even during the first year of reading instruction. Whatever the validity of these findings, their relationship to the child's progress in initial reading instruction remains to be established.

Although lack of understanding of the reading task might have a negative effect upon initial reading acquisition there is no evidence to substantiate this hypothesis. Furthermore, the oral reading errors reported by both Biemiller (1970) and Weber (1970) for beginning readers could be interpreted as evidence against this position. In both of these studies, even the poor readers, when they made substitution errors, did so in a manner that tended to retain a meaningful interpretation of the sentence through the point where the error was made. In the Weber study, for example, almost 90% of the substitution errors of both good and poor readers were in this category. Whatever misconceptions these children had about reading, one factor that they had clearly grasped was that the print was to be translated into meaningful utterances. Either the child's reported misunderstanding of the reading task results from the experimental methodology employed and is therefore not relevant to learning to read, or it is so minor a factor that it has no noticeable influence on the child once he or she encounters formal reading instruction. In either case, it is difficult to build a strong case for misunderstanding of the task as a major factor in reading failure.

Language Development   Although children come to the reading task with differing experiences and expectations, almost all can use language to communicate with adults and with peers. Articulation errors, although still occurring at the age of 6, particularly for English fricatives, result mostly from slow motor development and are not direct indicators of reading problems. Phonemic discrimination is also well developed at the first grade level, as adequate testing will reveal, even for those children so cavalierly classed as "verbally deprived." Morphology, syntax, and vocabulary continue to develop beyond this level, yet all three are already sufficiently developed to allow children to express their immediate needs and impressions. Reading problems related to morphology, syntax, and vocabulary may result, however, from the failure of reading texts to accurately reflect the level of development of each of these skills at various ages.

The child's ability to use language for communication presents mostly tactical problems for the teaching of reading—

selection of appropriate language forms and designation of which words must be taught orally before instruction begins. But the child's ability to treat language analytically is a far more serious problem, and has been identified as a crucial reading variable in a number of different cultures. At some point in almost all reading programs, sounds are treated as individual units that the child must manipulate, especially in attaching sounds to letters and blending them into words. These tasks are, for reasons still not understood, difficult for many children at the kindergarten and first grade levels. Zhurova (1963) reported that Russian children still have trouble at the age of seven in isolating the initial sound of a word, especially if the sound is a stop. Bruce (1964) tested British children on their ability to remove a medial sound from a word to produce a second word (e.g., the elimination of /t/ from *stand* to give *sand*) and found that below the age of seven they could not learn the task. Schenk-Danzinger (1967) reported similar results in Austria, as did Calfee, Chapman, and Venezky (1972) in the United States. Similarly, blending has been found to be difficult for some initial readers (Chall, Roswell, and Blumenthal, 1963).

In all of these studies, however, conclusions were reached on the basis of at most a few brief training/testing sessions, or a single testing session alone. Bruce, for example, presented a total of 30 test items in a single session with only a few warm-up items on which feedback was given. When carefully developed, sustained instruction is provided, most kindergarten level children prove capable of learning to match words according to their initial sounds and to blend sounds to make words (Kamm et al., 1974). Thus the inabilities may in fact be real, but they do not seem to indicate major deficits in processing capability so much as differences in acoustical experiences.

Perceptual and Cognitive Skills   For the average child the perceptual and cognitive demands of initial reading instruction, other than sound abstraction, are not excessive. At the kindergarten level children can match letters of the alphabet, although left-right reversals for single letters (e.g., the confusion of lower case *b* and *d*) and order reversals for letter strings (e.g., the confusion of *was* and *saw*) are common. These reversals may continue through first and even second grade, but are not by themselves barriers to learning to read, except in extremely rare cases. Most other skills required for learning initial reading—scanning left-to-right, following simple instructions, etc.—seem to be available by the end of kindergarten, even in children from lower socioeconomic environments. A few skills, however, such as those associated with sound manipulation and word identification, are often lacking in children of lower socioeconomic status.

Other Potential Skills Conspicuously missing from the skills mentioned above are, among others, letter-name knowledge, fine motor performance, and visual discrimination of objects and shapes—all skills that are prominent features of popular readiness programs and are assessed on standardized reading readiness tests (e.g., Metropolitan, Clymer-Barrett). There is strong evidence that training in these skills yields little gain in reading scores. Gates, Bond, and Russell (1939) found that at the primary level the correlation of geometric form perception with reading achievement was significantly lower than the correlation of word perception with reading. Paradis (1974) reported a series of studies in which reading achievement at the primary level was little affected by discrimination training with nonverbal stimuli.

Letter naming is central to the popular conception of reading instruction, but a logical justification for this role has never been made. According to Durrell (1956), letter names are effective mediators for letter sounds—a position rendered indefensible by a cursory glance at the alphabet. Three letters—*h, w,* and *y*—have names that do not contain their primary sounds and seven others—*a, e, i, o, u, c,* and *g*—do not contain the sound that is typically taught first in reading programs. Of the remaining 16, nine are composed of a consonant-vowel structure and seven are vowel-consonant (e.g., *f, l, m,* and *n*). This means that 40% of the letter names are not usable as sound mediators and the remaining 60% must be differentiated according to where the mediated sound occurs. There are, as most reading teachers know, more effective approaches to teaching letter sounds. It should also be pointed out that there is no evidence that instruction in letter naming improves reading achievement. Both Ohnmacht (1969) and Johnson (1970) failed to find a significant advantage in letter-name training over other forms of initial training for benefitting first grade reading achievement.

Fine motor training is in the same position as letter naming; it possesses neither a strong logical connection to reading nor experimental justification. On the contrary, attempts to affect initial reading skills through fine motor training have failed both with alphabetic (Pryzwansky, 1972) and nonalphabetic materials (Rosen, 1966; Cohen, 1967).

Acquisition of Initial Reading Skills

Letter-Sound Generalizations   Letter-sound generalizations are important for learning to read alphabetic or syllabic writing systems, although their use does not by itself guarantee competent reading behavior. Besides the roles they may play in the early processing stages of word recognition, they also aid the learner in developing word recognition ability by providing a means for: 1) checking the identification of a word previously encountered, but still not known well enough to be identified with high confidence from its components or from context; and 2) generating the pronunciations of words not encountered before in print, but that may be in the reader's listening vocabulary. Perfectly predictable correspondences are not required for either of these functions, because in each situation the reader has other cues to work with; the pronunciation of the printed form must only approximate in most circumstances the actual pronunciation for the appropriate match to be made. For example, in the sentence "The cowboy ran the horse into the street" the word *ran* may, if not recognized correctly by sight or context, be pronounced /ren/ initially, but if the reader has correctly interpreted "the cowboy" (and speaks English) he will probably recognize that this is not the correct form and try another pronunciation. Observations of children during oral reading show exactly this process at work. Without the ability to approximate sound from spelling, the child would be dependent upon other readers for substantiating his word identifications and consequently would develop this ability quite slowly.

Reliance on letter-sound generalizations in word recognition decreases as word identification ability increases, and the competent reader probably makes little use of them in normal reading. Nevertheless, the ability to apply letter-sound generalizations continues to develop at least through grade eight (Calfee, Venezky, and Chapman, 1969). Whether this is due to a continual reliance upon sounding out words or is a result of increasingly more efficient memory organization and retrieval is not known. But because the use of letter-sound generalizations seems to depend heavily upon examples stored in memory, organization and retrieval probably account for a significant part of this development.

Acquisitions of Specific Patterns The development of letter-sound generalizations has been studied over the past five years through the analysis of pronunciations of synthetic words constructed to contain specific spelling patterns (Calfee, Venezky, and Chapman, 1969; Venezky, Chapman, and Calfee, 1972; Venezky and Johnson, 1973; Perfetti and Hogaboam, 1975). Results from these studies are primarily descriptive, either of age or reading ability differences, or of relationships between decoding ability and other reading abilities (e.g., comprehension). Some of the results, however, are suggestive of how information is processed during decoding, and of the effects of instruction upon this process. The more important of these, drawn from Venezky, Chapman, and Calfee, 1972, are summarized below (see also Venezky, 1974).

Completeness of Processing Good and poor readers at the second grade level differed little in their ability to decode invariant consonants (e.g., b, d, l, and m) at the beginning of words. (Both groups scored above 90% correct.) However, for the same consonants in medial and final position, the poorer readers showed a dramatic drop in percentage of correct responses while the better readers showed only a slight reduction. The initial position scores for the poorer readers indicate that neither the concept of attaching sounds to specific letters nor the particular letter-sound correspondences involved in the study were major sources of difficulty. What was troublesome was the processing of information beyond the first letter of a word. One hypothesis is that all of the letters are processed, at least through recognition, but in generating a pronunciation only the sound correspondences for the initial letters are consistently applied. Correspondences for some of the remaining letters might be applied, especially for vowels, but generating a "word" that sounds English might be sufficient to satisfy the poorer reader.

An alternative hypothesis is that some of the letters after the initial ones are not processed properly, that is, they are incorrectly recognized, but correspondences are applied for all of the resulting identifications. A forced-choice letter recognition task might provide a test for these hypotheses, but the possibility of a strategy change by the reader for such a task would need to be considered.

The Role of Exemplars   The complexity of a correspondence, computed from the number and type of graphemic, morphemic, and phonological features that need to be considered for proper application, is not a good predictor of how quickly a correspondence is acquired. Single-letter vowel spellings in monosyllabic words, for example, can be either short or long, depending (in general) upon whether the word ends with a consonant or with a final *e*. To generalize this rule, a child must observe not only the letter that follows the vowel but also the letter after that. For initial *c*, on the other hand, the child need check only the following letter. If it is *e*, *i*, or *y*, the *c* is soft as in *cent*, *city*, and *cycle*; otherwise it is hard as in *clip*, *coat*, *crumb*, and *cute*.

The initial *c* patterns have only one exception among the words that grade schoolers might see—*cello*—and this word is rare in the primary grades. The long-short patterns, on the other hand, have numerous common exceptions (e.g., *cold*, *axe*, *pint*, *won*, *wash*, and *one*), yet the percentage of correct responses to the long-short patterns at the fourth grade level was more than twice that of *c* before *e*, *i*, or *y* (86% vs. 41%).

Both the long-short distinction and the *c* before *e*, *i*, or *y* pattern are taught in one way or another in most reading programs prior to the fourth grade, but one important difference can be noted from an inspection of the vocabularies that reading programs emphasize. Words for both long and short patterns are numerous, and are often minimally contrastive, (e.g., *mat*—*mate*, *rip*—*ripe*). Words with *c* before *e*, *i*, or *y*, on the other hand, are rare before fourth grade, and represent probably less than 10% of all the initial *c* words introduced. What constitutes a sufficient number of exemplars to induce a generalization has not been explored extensively for any language pattern, yet clearly it should be a major concern for instruction.

Failure to Generalize   As the child encounters more and more exemplars for soft initial *c*, he begins to acquire the appropriate response for this pattern; however, both eighth graders and college students did not exceed 70% correct response. The responses to a related pattern, that of *g* before *e*, *i*, or *y*, also demonstrated an exemplar affect, but here the effect was one of

complete non-generalization. For stimulus words in which initial
g should, in theory, be soft (that is, g before e, or i in the present
study), fewer than 25% of the responses at any grade level (2, 4, 6,
or 8) were correct, almost all of the incorrect responses being
hard g (/g/).

What might be responsible for this lack of generalization
are both the number of high frequency words that are exceptions
to the so-called rule (e.g., *get*, *geese*, *gear*, *gift*, *girl*, and *give*),
and the lack of sufficient rule-observing exemplars. (Among the
high frequency words used in initial reading, only *gem*, *general*,
germ, *giant*, and *ginger* have a soft initial g). Encountering other
rule-observing words in reading beyond the primary or elementary levels does not seem to have much effect on the generalization of this pattern, because only 25% of the college student
responses for g before e and i were correct. It may be that there is
a critical stage for the formation of letter-sound correspondences,
or, equally plausible, perhaps only the more frequently occurring English words have an effect upon generalization processes.

Visual Word Recognition   What little is known about the
development of visual word recognition derives from about a
dozen studies that have been reported over the last 40 years. In
the earliest "modern" study on this topic, Hill (1936) established
that the main effect of reading instruction was to focus the
learner's attention on the beginning of the word. Hill also found
(as have a number of studies since) that even in the earliest
stages of learning, word configuration is not a salient cue for
recognition.

Attempts to isolate the cues that children use in recognition
at different stages of learning (Gates and Boeker, 1923; Marchbanks and Levin, 1965; Williams, Blumberg, and Williams,
1970; Leslie, 1975) have generally been restricted to the prereading and early primary reading stages. In general, these studies
have supported Hill's findings, especially regarding the saliency
of the first letters of a word.

A second and potentially more important line of recent research has been in the development of awareness of orthographic
structure. Much of this work derives from E. J. Gibson's studies
of recognition of pronounceable and unpronounceable nonsense
words, but the general conclusion from several different studies
is that at least by the third year of reading instruction, children
can demonstrate an awareness of orthographic regularity
(Rosinski and Wheeler, 1972; Golinkoff, 1974).

This result is especially important when viewed in relation to two other research trends. One of these trends is represented by word recognition studies that use adult subjects, and especially those studies that attempt to isolate processing stages. Orthographic structure seems to be a major variable in the recognition process, particularly for explaining why a letter can be identified more rapidly in a word than in isolation. (For a summary of recent work in this area, see Massaro, 1975, and Gibson and Levin, 1975.) The picture that is emerging of the word recognition process gives a central role to knowledge of orthographic structure in the earlier stages.

The second trend is represented by developmental studies of visual information processing, but especially those by Haith and his students on the role of short-term visual memory in the processing of geometric forms (Haith, 1971). These studies suggest that the basic differences between children and adults in visual information processing lie in the utilization of experience and familiarity for storage, encoding, and visual rehearsal. Children and adults did not differ significantly in threshold recognition times for single stimuli presented at the center of the visual field, nor did five-year-olds show any decrease in recognition ability for stimuli exposed three degrees off center. When multiple stimuli were presented in a single array, with an indication of the item to report appearing at variable times after the offset of the array, children and adults showed the same rate of decrease in accuracy for delays of up to 150 msec. After that point, however, the five-year-olds did significantly worse than the adults.

What these results suggest for the study of reading acquisition is that basic visual processing capabilities are already developed by the time the child encounters the reading task. But what must develop is an ability to store briefly the stimuli in reading, that is, words and word components, until recognition and integration take place. The most relevant experience for aiding this process, given the lack of saliency of word configuration, centers on orthographic structure. It seems, therefore, that the most promising research on the acquisition of word recognition ability is that which explores the role of orthographic structure in recognition and storage.

It should be pointed out, however, that the concept of orthographic structure is still somewhat vague. The first attempt to relate orthographic structure to word perception (Gibson et al., 1962) concluded that the relevant perceptual units were letter clusters with relatively invariant mappings into sound. However, a replication of this study with deaf subjects (Gibson, Shurcliff, and Yonas, 1970) showed that the mapping into sound was not essential for facilitation of word recognition.

In the current literature on word recognition two approaches to describing intra-word redundancy can be found: statistical re- dundancy approaches (e.g., summed digram or trigram counts); and rule governed regularity approaches (see Venezky and Mas- saro, 1978, in press). How these relate to each other and to word recognition is only now being explored (cf. Massaro, Venezky, and Taylor, 1978, in press).

Summary   The research on letter-sound learning to date has concentrated on establishing developmental norms for par- ticular letter-sound patterns. This has important applications for reading instruction, but leaves unanswered the question of what processing mechanisms are utilized in developing such generalizations and how they relate to knowledge of ortho- graphic structure. As mentioned earlier, work with deaf subjects indicates that orthographic structure is not necessarily depen- dent on letter-sound generalizations (Gibson, Shurcliff, and Yonas, 1970); however, the relationships between these two areas remain to be explored for hearing subjects. Because almost all approaches to reading instruction employ overt teaching of letter-sound correspondences, a thorough understanding of their acquisition and utilization merits a high priority in developmen- tal research.

CONCLUSIONS

What should be concluded from this review is that reading ac- quisition is neither occult nor obscure. Organizational and man- agement variables, such as leadership, teacher training, and diagnosis, seem to be more important determinants of reading success than do specific instructional methods, and should there- fore be the focus of instructional research. From what has been learned since the earliest studies on reading, there is no justifica- tion for a continued research emphasis on the so-called methods of reading instruction or on modified alphabets. There is clearly a need for good reading programs, and these remarks should not be interpreted as opposition to program development and dissemination, although most of what has appeared in the last five years from commercial publishers has been minor perturbations around well-worn themes. However, with the breakdown of the teacher-centered, self-contained classroom, coordination and training of staff and management of large numbers of students engaged in diverse reading activities become essential, and it is on these processes that instructional research is especially needed.

For research aimed at a basic understanding of how reading is acquired, certain directions are strongly justifiable. The most important of these is research on orthographic regularity, including the relationship of orthographic regularity to letter-sound generalizations. Many questions remain unanswered about prerequisites to learning to read, about eye movements, and obviously about comprehension, but given the current directions of experimental psychology and the present needs of instruction, the most fundamental gap in our understanding of how reading is acquired is in the development of word recognition ability.

Within the current state of understanding of visual information processing, the role of orthographic structure appears to be the most crucial factor that needs to be resolved. An extreme hypothesis which might be advanced is that the most important change that the child undergoes in learning to read, and perhaps the only major change that is unique to reading, is in his knowledge of orthographic structure. This structure is possibly the basis for rapid letter and word recognition and thus essential for allowing processing capacity for semantic integration. This latter ability develops primarily from listening experiences but must be related to the internal form of words derived from visual input for reading to take place.

The importance of these conclusions rests not in the particular topics themselves, but in the assumption that enough is known about reading acquisition to select certain topics as highly important for advancing our ability to instruct and to reject others as marginal or distractive. Wide agreement on the selection is not anticipated, but we should be satisfied if the opposition to these conclusions is based upon both a thorough and comprehensive review of the research findings and the assumption that, even considering the gaps in our knowledge about reading acquisition, the subject is far from mysterious.

REFERENCES

Biemiller, A. 1970. The development of the use of graphic and contextual information as children learn to read. Reading Research Quarterly 6:75−96.

Bloomfield, L. 1933. Language. New York: Holt, Rinehart and Winston.

Bond, G. L., and Dykstra, R. 1967. The cooperative research program in first-grade reading instruction. Reading Research Quarterly 2:5−142.

Bruce, D. J. 1964. The analysis of word sounds by young children. British Journal of Educational Psychology 31:158−169.

Burroughs, E. R. 1963. Tarzan of the Apes. New York: Ballantine Books. (First published in 1912.)

Calfee, R., Chapman, R., and Venezky, R. 1972. How a child needs to think to learn to read. In L. W. Gregg (ed.), Cognition in Learning and Memory. New York: John Wiley & Sons.

Calfee, R., Venezky, R., and Chapman, R. 1969. Pronunciation of synthetic words with predictable and unpredictable letter-sound correspondences. Technical Report No. 71. Madison: Wisconsin Research and Development Center for Cognitive Learning.

Chall, J. S., Roswell, F. G., and Blumenthal, S. H. 1963. Auditory blending ability: a factor in success in beginning reading. Reading Teacher 17:113−118.

Cohen, R. 1967. Remedial training of first grade children with visual perceptual retardation. Educational Horizons 45:60−63.

Downing, J. 1973. Comparative Reading. New York: The Macmillan Co.

Durrell, D. D. 1956. Improving Reading Instruction. New York: World Book Co.

Flanders, N. A. 1970. Analyzing Classroom Interactions. New York: Addison-Wesley Publishing Co.

Gates, A. I., and Boeker, E. 1923. A study of initial stages in reading by pre-school children. Teachers College Record 24:469−488.

Gates, A. I., Bond, G. L., and Russell, D. H. 1939. Methods of Determining Reading Readiness. New York: Teachers College Press, Columbia University.

Gibson, E. J., and Levin, H. 1975. The Psychology of Reading. Cambridge, Mass.: M.I.T. Press.

Gibson, E. J., Pick, A., Osser, H., and Hammond, M. 1962. Role of grapheme-phoneme correspondence in perception of words. American Journal of Psychology 75:554−570.

Gibson, E. J., Shurcliff, A., and Yonas, A. 1970. Utilization of spelling patterns by deaf and hearing subjects. In H. Levin and J. P. Williams (eds.), Basic Studies on Reading. New York: Basic Books.

Golinkoff, R. M. 1974. Children's discrimination of English spelling patterns with redundant auditory information. Paper presented at a meeting of the American Educational Research Association, Chicago.

Haith, M. M. 1971. Developmental changes in visual information processing and short-term visual memory. Human Development 14:249−261.

Hill, M. B. 1936. A study of the process of word discrimination in individuals beginning to read. Journal of Educational Research 29:487−500.

Johnson, D. 1970. Factors related to the pronunciation of vowel clusters. Technical Report No. 149. Madison: Wisconsin Research and Development Center for Cognitive Learning.

Kamm, M. et al. 1974. The 1971–72 field test of the Prereading Skills Program. Technical Report No. 269. Madison: Wisconsin Research and Development Center for Cognitive Learning.

Klausmeier, H. J., Rossmiller, R. A., and Saily, M. 1977. Individually Guided Elementary Education. New York: Academic Press.

Leslie, R. 1975. Position saliency in children's short-term recognition memory for graphic patterns. Technical Report No. 351. Madison: Wisconsin Research and Development Center for Cognitive Learning.

Marchbanks, G., and Levin, H. 1965. Cues by which children recognize words. Journal of Educational Psychology 56:57–61.

Massaro, D. (ed.) 1975. Understanding Language: An Information Processing Analysis of Speech Perception, Reading, and Psycholinguistics. New York: Academic Press.

Massaro, D. W., Venezky, R. L., and Taylor, G. A. Orthographic regularity, positional frequency, and visual processing of letter strings. Journal of Experimental Psychology-General (in press).

Mayakovsky, V. 1960. The Bedbug and Selected Poetry. (M. Hayward and G. Reavy, trans.; P. Blake, ed.) New York: Meridian Books. (Originally published 1955–1958.)

Ohnmacht, D. C. 1969. The effects of letter knowledge on achievement in reading in the first grade. Paper presented at the meeting of the American Educational Research Association, February 7, Los Angeles.

Paradis, E. E. 1974. The appropriateness of visual discrimination exercises in reading readiness materials. Journal of Educational Research 67:276–278.

Perfetti, C. A., and Hogaboam, T. 1975. The relationship between single word decoding and reading comprehension skill. Journal of Educational Psychology 67:461–469.

Pitman, J. 1961. Learning to read. Reprinted from the February Journal of the Royal Society of Arts.

Pryzwansky, W. B. 1972. Effects of perceptual-motor training and manuscript writing on reading readiness skills in kindergarten. Journal of Educational Psychology 63:110–115.

Quilling, M. R., and Otto, W. 1971. Evaluation of an objective-based curriculum in reading. Journal of Educational Psychology 65:15–18.

Reid, J. F. 1966. Learning to think about reading. Educational Research 9:56–62.

Rosen, C. 1966. An experimental study of visual perceptual training and reading achievement in first grade. Perceptual and Motor Skills 22:979–986.

Rosinski, R. R., and Wheeler, K. E. 1972. Children's use of orthographic structure in word recognition. Psychonomic Science 26:97–98.

Schenk-Danzinger, L. 1967. Probleme der Legasthenie. Schweizerische Zeitschrift für Psychologie 20:29–48.

State of New York, Office of Education Performance Review. 1974.

School Factors Influencing Reading Achievement; A Case Study of Two Inner City Schools. Albany, New York.

Venezky, R. L. 1974. Theoretical and experimental bases for teaching reading. In T. A. Sebeok (ed.), Current Trends in Linguistics, volume 12. The Hague: Mouton.

Venezky, R. L. 1977. Research on reading processes: an historical perspective. American Psychologist 32:339–345.

Venezky, R. L. 1978. Two approaches to reading assessment: a comparison of apples and oranges. In S. Pflaum-Conner (ed.), Aspects of Reading Education. Berkeley, Ca.: McCutchan Publishing Corp.

Venezky, R. L., Chapman, R. S., and Calfee, R. C. 1972. The development of letter-sound generalizations from second through sixth grade. Technical Report No. 231. Madison: Wisconsin Research and Development Center for Cognitive Learning.

Venezky, R. L., and Johnson, D. 1973. Development of two letter-sound patterns in grades one through three. Journal of Educational Psychology 64:109–115.

Venezky, R. L., and Massaro, D. W. The role of orthographic regularity in word recognition. In L. Resnick and P. Weaver (eds.), Theory and Practice of Early Reading. Hillsdale, N.J.: Erlbaum Associates (in press).

Weber, G. 1971. Inner-city children can be taught to read: four successful schools. Occasional Paper No. 18, Washington, D. C.: Council for Basic Education.

Weber, R. M. 1970. First graders use of grammatical context in reading. In H. Levin and J. Williams (eds.), Basic Studies on Reading. New York: Harper and Row.

Williams, J. P., Blumberg, E. L., and Williams, D. V. 1970. Cues used in visual word recognition. Journal of Educational Psychology 61:310–315.

Zhurova, L. E. 1963. The development of analysis of words into sounds by preschool children. Soviet Psychology and Psychiatry 2:17–27. (Published originally in Russian in Voprosy Psikhology, No. 3, 1963.)

CRITIQUE:
Phonemic Awareness Skills and Reading Achievement
Roberta Michnick Golinkoff*

Many authors have discussed the difficulty young prereading children have with segmenting individual spoken words into their phonemic elements (e.g., Calfee, Chapman, and Venezky, 1972; Gleitman and Rozin, 1973; Liberman, 1973; Gibson and Levin, 1975; Fox and Routh, 1976; Wallach and Wallach, 1976). A number of studies have reported data on the relationship between such segmentation skills and reading achievement (e.g., Rosner and Simon, 1971; Liberman, 1973; Fox and Routh, 1975; Goldstein, 1976). In addition, there now exist studies that have attempted to teach segmentation skills (e.g., Venezky, Green, and Leslie, 1975; Marsh and Mineo, 1977) and to observe the relationship between this training and reading achievement (Rosner, 1971; Wallach and Wallach, 1976). Although Venezky (this volume) suggests that the absence of these segmentation skills does not present a major stumbling block in the acquisition of reading skill because they can be readily developed through training, the purpose of this chapter is to examine some of the available data on this issue. Because Calfee, Lindamood, and Lindamood (1973) report, for example, an impressive relationship between segmentation skills and reading achievement through grade 12, segmentation skills may merit more attention from researchers than Venezky implies in the previous chapter.

To paraphrase a recent title (Calfee, Chapman, and Venezky, 1972), what does a child need to know to learn how to read? In addition to being able to speak the language, to discriminate between the alphabet's orthographic units, and to associate letter and letter groups with their characteristic sounds (Gibson, 1970), the ability to segment individual spoken words into their component sounds is necessary. Reading words constructed from an

* I wish to thank Dr. Jerome Rosner (now at the University of Houston) and Dr. Phyllis Weaver (now at Harvard University) both formerly of the Learning Research and Development Center at the University of Pittsburgh, for innumerable interesting discussions on many of the issues in this paper.

alphabet (as opposed to a syllabary) involves the recognition that the letters on the page can be deciphered by first analyzing the sounds of which they are composed, and then blending these sounds together. But as numerous authors have now concluded (e.g., Savin, 1972; Liberman et al., 1974; Venezky, 1976; Gleitman and Rozin, 1977; Rozin and Gleitman, 1977), the segmentation and synthesis of the phonemic units that compose spoken words is no easy task. This is due to two factors. First, segmentation and synthesis require children to become aware of the abstract units of which their speech is composed. As Gleitman and Rozin (1977) put it, ". . . learning to read requires a rather explicit and conscious discovery and building from what one already knows implicitly for the sake of speech: the structure of one's language and, particularly, the sound structure of one's language" (p. 3). Seen in a developmental context it is not surprising that preschoolers have trouble becoming conscious of elements of their language. In recent years developmental psychologists have become most absorbed in the issue of how young children become aware of and utilize their memory capabilities (see Flavell, 1977, for a review of this literature). The parallels between these areas are obvious: children do, quite clearly, use language in everyday speech and remember large quantities of information. And yet, externalizing this knowledge and being able to treat the knowledge system in question as an object does not follow automatically on the heels of use of the system.

The second factor, as research by Liberman et al. (1967) has shown, is that there is often no acoustic criterion for deciding where one phoneme ends in a word and another begins. Thus, consciously separating the sounds of a word is a difficult and artificial task. The final product of segmentation often sounds very little like the original word because the separate consonant sounds produced (except in the case of continuants) have an extra *schwa* sound. For example, the word *dot* when segmented would sound like *duh —o —tuh*. Consonants pronounced in isolation do not sound the same as they do in context. Unless the child is aware of the fact that the phonemic segments of a word are only imprecise and abstract analogues of the way these phonemes sound in the word, the task of pronouncing words not read before is a difficult one.

Reading a new one-syllable word requires first, that the word be broken (analyzed, segmented) into its component phonemes and second, that the resulting units be recombined (blended or synthesized). It is possible that the auditory analogues of these analysis and synthesis skills are separate abilities that ordinarily enter a child's repertoire successively. On logical grounds it would seem that before a child could recognize or blend a word from its separate phonemic elements, the child would have to know that a word can be analyzed into separate parts. Thus, perhaps in its natural acquisition, segmentation precedes synthesis. There has been no study that compares segmentation and synthesis skills in the same children—even at the level of word units or syllables. Goldstein (1976) gave analysis and synthesis tasks to his subjects but does not present the data on these tasks separately.

In order to say an individual possesses phonemic segmentation and synthesis skills, what should s/he be able to do? What is a reasonable operational definition of the presence or absence of these skills? This question is not as straightforward as it may first seem to be. By now researchers have come up with a number of tasks to assess this knowledge. For example, some have asked children to produce rhymes (Calfee, Chapman, and Venezky, 1972), to say which of two words start with a given initial sound (Wallach et al., 1977), to replace a sound in a word with another sound (Bruce, 1964) and to represent the separate sounds of a word with a clap or a tap on the table or a dash or by placing a counter or poker chip (Rosner, 1969; Holden and MacGinitie, 1972; Liberman et al., 1974). Using the same or similar tasks, researchers have also explored children's sensitivity to sentence and syllabic units. As differentiation theory (Gibson, 1969) would predict, sentences are easier to segment into words than words are to segment into syllables and both sentence and syllable segmentation are easier than phoneme segmentation— even when task demands are minimized (Fox and Routh, 1975). (See Gibson and Levin, 1975, for a review of much of this literature.)

In much the same way that Rosner (1969) organized the tasks in his auditory analysis training program, the research tasks in the literature can be represented in a two-dimensional matrix. A given task's level of difficulty could be predicted by where it falls in the matrix. One dimension in the matrix would be the unit to be analyzed (sentence into words, words into syllables, syllables into phonemes). The other dimension would be the operation to be performed on the unit. An analysis of the cognitive processes required to perform a given task would yield a hierarchy of tasks. For example, recognizing the presence or absence of a unit should be easier than adding or deleting the element oneself. Performing a deletion and recombining the remaining elements should be easier than performing the deletion and replacing the deleted element with another element. A third dimension—the number of units to be operated on—is suggested by studies that indicate that the more elements to be operated on, the harder the task (e.g., Goldstein, 1976). The work of Rosner (1969) provides some validation for this ordering of tasks, as do the ages reported in the literature for when children are able to perform various of these tasks. Training could also be expected to modify the difficulty level of any unit/task combination.

In the literature, some studies have used very stringent measures of phonemic awareness, and others have used much lower level tasks to make the same judgment. For example, Bruce (1964) used phoneme replacement and Wallach et al. (1977) used a recognition task. In summary, a minimal level of phonemic analysis skill could be operationally defined as being able to recognize that a word begins with a given sound. A minimal level of synthesis skill would be being able to recognize the word that someone else's segmented sounds make. However, as will be seen below, tasks in the literature require a wider range of segmentation and synthesis abilities.

In the following sections, the relationship between phonemic segmentation skills and reading achievement will be examined. First, correlational studies will be reviewed, followed by experimental studies, and finally by research on training these skills.

CORRELATIONAL STUDIES

A number of researchers have assessed children's competence on phonemic segmentation tasks and correlated these scores with scores on tests of reading achievement. Some authors have used standardized reading instruments and some have used performance on reading tests they designed. In some studies, the presence or absence of phonemic awareness skills has been examined in light of other prereading skills. The literature suggests that children who do not have phonemic awareness skills may often have a number of other prereading skills. It is worth considering what skills may be present even in the absence of phonemic awareness.

First, as stated above, preschoolers have been using language for several years before entering the reading situation. A lack of phonemic awareness does not mean a lack of phonemic discrimination, as Wallach et al. (1977) have shown in an experiment with prereading kindergartners from lower- and middle-class socioeconomic backgrounds. In the past, some authors have argued that children of low socioeconomic backgrounds failed at reading because they lacked elementary phonemic discrimination skills (e.g., Deutsch, 1964). As a test of phonemic discrimination, Wallach et al. presented children with pairs of pictures whose names differed only by their initial phoneme, e.g., *whale* and *jail.* Children were asked to point to the picture the experimenter then named. Both middle- and lower-class children had no problem with this task, getting practically all items correct. Three sorts of phonemic awareness tasks were used, all involving analysis skills and all relatively simple tasks. For example, in one task, the experimenter showed the child two pairs of pictures with maximally contrasting names, *man* and *house,* and asked the child to point to the picture that starts with the /m/ sound. Wallach, et al. found that on each of the three phonemic analysis tasks, "most of the middle-class children scored at or near the maximum possible, while most of the disadvantaged children earned low scores" (1977:38). Thus, phonemic discrimination skills are independent of and precede phonemic awareness skills.

Second, researchers have observed that children who lack phonemic awareness skills can discriminate between the letters and even give the letter sounds. Liberman (1973) wrote that reading-disabled children have been observed to give the sounds of the letters, but when shown a word and asked to read it, they continually produce a nonsense word that is a combination of the segments, e.g., *buh−ah−tuh* for *bat.* Apparently, many critical prereading skills can be in a child's repertoire even though phonemic awareness is not one of them.

Other studies have examined the relationship between phonemic awareness skills and reading achievement. Rosner and Simon (1971) gave the "Auditory Analysis Test," a test that required syllable and phoneme deletion, to children from kindergarten through sixth grade. A sample syllable item was, "Say *birthday*. Now say it again without the *day*." A sample phoneme item was, "Say *belt*. Now say it again without *l*." In all cases the remaining unit was a real word. The correlations between performance on the Language Arts section of the Stanford Achievement Test and on the Auditory Analysis Test were significant and ranged from a low of $r = 0.53$ in kindergarten to a high of $r = 0.84$ in third grade.

Liberman et al. (1974) used a tapping task to test their prediction that syllabic segmentation would be easier for children than phonemic segmentation. Children in preschool, kindergarten, and first grade were trained to tap a small wooden dowel on a table for each segment in the one-, two-, or three-syllable word that was the stimulus item. The investigators found steady improvement with age in producing the correct number of taps for syllables and phonemes, with phoneme segmentation always significantly more difficult. For example, in the first grade, only 70% of the children reached criterion on the phoneme segmentation task, while 90% were successful in the syllable task. Liberman (1973) reported these same first-grader results on the Wide Range Achievement Test given several months later when these children were in second grade. These data supported the relationship between phoneme segmentation skill and reading ability; half of the children in the lowest third of the class in reading had failed the phoneme segmentation task but none of the children in the top third in reading failed it.

Calfee, Lindamood, and Lindamood (1973) studied the relationship between performance in the Lindamood Auditory Conceptualization Test (Lindamood and Lindamood, 1971) and performance on the Wide Range Achievement Test (WRAT) for grades kindergarten through twelve. The Lindamood test requires subjects to use colored blocks to stand for identities and relationships among spoken sounds. For example, for the sound sequences /s−s−n/, the subject could select two blocks of the same color and one of a different color, e.g., green−green−yellow. These authors found that when a combination of WRAT reading and spelling scores were used in a multiple regression analysis, more than 50% of the total variance in reading ability at all grades could be predicted from performance on the Lindamood test.

Fox and Routh (1975) used a procedure that coaxed subjects to engage in as much sentence, syllable, and phoneme segmentation as they possibly could. They repeatedly asked their three-to seven-year-old subjects to "Tell me a little bit of what I just said," and rewarded them with raisins. They re-presented initially unanalyzed segments until the children had analyzed them into the smallest units they could. Even with their coaxing, phoneme segmentation was significantly harder than syllable or sentence segmentation. Phoneme segmentation also correlated significantly ($r = 0.50$, $p < 0.01$) with performance on the Peabody Individual Achievement Test in Reading Recognition. The Peabody Test did not correlate as highly with sentence segmentation ($r = 0.31$, $p < 0.05$) or syllable segmentation ($r = 0.29$, $p > 0.05$).

Calfee (1977) cited a study by Calfee (1972) that reported that phonemic segmentation scores of subjects when they were in kindergarten "contributed substantially to the multiple regression equation predicting reading achievement [in the first grade]; this contribution was over and above the total test score for all skills combined" (Calfee, 1977:314).

In summary, a number of studies report significant correlations between phonemic segmentation skills and reading achievement. As with any set of correlational data, the inferences to be made here are limited. For example, do segmentation skills covary with some third factor, say IQ? If they do, IQ differences may be responsible for these significant correlations. Although IQ may correlate with phonemic awareness skills, these skills seem to make an independent contribution to reading achievement. The results of Rosner and Simon (1971) bear on this point. Rosner and Simon also performed a correlation between Stanford Achievement Test Language Arts section scores and scores on the Auditory Analysis Test, partialling out IQ. All the partial correlations remained significant except for that of the sixth grade group. As a conservative research tactic, however, IQ should continue to be controlled in studies.

As in any correlational study, the direction, if any, of causation is unclear. Another question is, are phonemic segmentation abilities necessary for reading success or does learning to read cause the child to acquire phonemic segmentation skills? Some of the studies discussed below were directed at this issue, although none presents an air-tight case. This may be because the causal arrow can go both ways. If a child does not have phonemic segmentation abilities prior to reading instruction, s/he may indeed do more poorly than a child who does. However, some children, either by virtue of the reading method they are learning with or an astute teacher or their own insight, may catch on to the phonemic concept as a function of reading instruction. For this reason, it may be difficult to make a clean case for the necessity of phonemic segmentation skills *prior* to reading instruction.

It is worth mentioning one more correlational study of a slightly different nature. Fowler, Liberman, and Shankweiler (1977) reasoned that if phoneme segmentation is a problem for many beginning readers, then more reading errors should be made on final consonants in consonant-vowel-consonant sequences than on initial consonants. This is because the initial sound is easiest to isolate and to relate to its orthographic representation than a medial or final sound that is embedded within the syllable and requires analysis. Their results confirmed their prediction. Subjects in the second through the fourth grade made significantly more errors on final than on initial consonants. Although this is an interesting finding given their theoretical analysis, a more compelling case for the role of phonemic analysis in reading errors could have been made if the authors had tested their subjects' ability to segment words orally. If phonemic segmentation skills were responsible for their results, then children with weak segmentation skills should have made disproportionately more errors on final segments than children with relatively strong segmentation skills.

EXPERIMENTAL STUDIES

Many researchers have trained children to perform various phonemic segmentation tasks (e.g., Elkonin, 1963, 1973; Venezky, Green and Leslie 1975), but only those who related their results to reading achievement will be discussed.

Goldstein (1976) was interested in two questions: first, would children who were more advanced relative to their peers on certain cognitive and linguistic skills learn more from reading instruction; and second, would reading instruction, in turn, stimulate these children's cognitive and linguistic skills? The skills he selected to study were segmentation and synthesis of syllables and phonemes and sequential memory ability. I will focus on the former—the segmentation and synthesis skills. Word synthesis skills were assessed by having the four-year-old subjects "guess" what the name of a "secret picture" was. The experimenter hid a picture and produced its name in segmented fashion like *kan −ga −roo* or *tuh −ea* (for *tea*). Segmentation was tested by asking children to segment a word or syllable the experimenter had previously segmented, or a new word. After these tests the children were randomly assigned to two groups, one of which received reading training while the other used the same storybooks to learn about letters and have the stories read to them. Reading achievement was measured by tests designed by the author. One test assessed subjects' ability to read isolated words and the other to read words in context, that is, stories. Unlike many "flash in the pan" training studies, this study's training period was 10 minutes each school day for 13 weeks. Also, the reliability of Goldstein's tests were high, all above $r = 0.78$.

Goldstein's results replicated the now reliable finding that segmentation and synthesis of syllabic units is significantly easier than the segmentation and synthesis of phonemic units. Also, the more segments (two vs. three) to be segmented or synthesized, the harder the task. What is most interesting is the finding that, independent of IQ, as tested in a regression analysis, word analysis-synthesis skill was a good predictor of reading achievement on both reading tests, but especially on the test of reading isolated words, where it accounted for about 56% of the variance.

As a result of reading instruction, word analysis-synthesis skill seemed to improve more for the experimental than for the control group. However, this result emerged only from an examination of the number of stimulus categories in which improvement was shown. The experimental group improved in all categories but three that involved phonemic analysis. The control group did poorest in the six categories involving phonemic analysis. Thus reading instruction does seem to improve word analysis and synthesis skills but more at the syllabic than the phonemic level. Also, those children in the experimental group whose scores on word analysis and synthesis were lowest before reading instruction showed the most improvement in their analysis-synthesis scores after reading instruction ($r = -0.92, p < 0.01$).

Thus the Goldstein (1976) findings indicate that segmentation skills can predict success in initial reading instruction. In turn, initial reading instruction seems to improve segmentation skills—at least at the syllabic level. Perhaps if the training program had continued, the children's phonemic analysis skills would have improved as well. The fact that the experimental group children improved their phonemic *synthesis* skills suggests that synthesis may be an easier skill and may be independent of analysis skill.

Fox and Routh (1976) were interested in the roles played by phonemic analysis and phonemic synthesis in the decoding of new words. To support their contention that blending or synthesizing individual sounds may need to be explicitly taught during reading instruction, they cited the work of Jeffrey and Samuels (1967), Muller (1972-1973), and Jenkins, Bausell, and Jenkins (1972) and unpublished work by Silberman. All these researchers reported that in their experiments phonic blend training was essential for children to profit from letter-sound training and to be able to read new words.

Fox and Routh (1976) first taught their four-year-old subjects to discriminate between Gibson's letter-like forms and to scan from left to right. Half of the children were randomly selected to receive individual phonic blend training. It turned out by chance that half of this group (as assessed at the end of the experiment) was capable of phonemic segmentation and half was not. Then all subjects learned a sound to associate with each letter-like form and learned to read two counterbalanced word lists composed of three words each. Criterion was two consecutive correct trials on a list or a maximum of twenty trials.

Interestingly, there was no main effect of phonic blending training but there was a main effect of segmentation ability. Children who were above the median in segmentation ability learned the first list in 12.60 trials. Children below the median could not read the list correctly within the twenty trials allotted. In addition, these groups differed significantly on the number of errors they made and on the number of words read correctly on the first trial of the first list. These results were, not surprisingly, replicated on the second list, given immediately after the first list. In summary, the ability to segment single syllable words into phonemes emerged again as a good predictor of reading achievement. Granted, the instructional period in this study was very brief (one 30-minute session) and the nonsegmenters might have, at some point, caught on to the task. However these results may indicate that phonemic segmentation skills are necessary for the earliest stages of reading instruction.

Although there was no main effect for phonic blending training, there was an interaction between phonic blending training and segmentation ability for reading performance on the second list. The children who were segmenters and had received blending training reached criterion on the second list in 9.3 trials as compared to a mean of 17.2 trials for the segmenters who had not been trained to blend. These findings suggest that blending training will only be helpful if some minimum threshold of segmentation ability has been reached. This may help to explain the Goldstein (1976) findings. Goldstein found that both his groups improved their segmentation and synthesis skills at the syllabic level and their synthesis skills at the phonemic level. Phonemic segmentation skills lagged even for the subjects more advanced in this general area at the start. Although Goldstein does not report his data separately for synthesis vs. analysis tasks, perhaps it can be assumed that the reason his subjects' synthesis skills improved was that they could engage in some phonemic segmentation. Both data sets imply that analysis and synthesis skills may be independently acquired.

IQ, or some other cognitive ability, as the hidden third factor cannot be dismissed, however. Fox and Routh (1976) did not control for IQ. As they stated:

> ... these findings are essentially correlational ones, and one might argue that it is some correlate of segmentation ability (for example, some more general cognitive aptitude) that is essential in this aspect of initial reading. Research needs to be carried out on methods of training children in segmenting. . . . If such training methods can be worked out, their effects on children's performance at decoding unfamiliar words can be studied (1976:73).

There are two studies reported in sufficient detail (unlike Elkonin, 1963; 1973) that did what Fox and Routh (1976) requested: children were trained to segment syllables into phonemes and the effect of this training on reading achievement was assessed (Rosner, 1971; Wallach and Wallach, 1976).

TRAINING STUDIES

Until recently many researchers (e.g., Gleitman and Rozin 1973) assumed that phonemic segmentation skills were not trainable. Now, however, many American psychologists have learned of the work of Russian psychologist D. B. Elkonin (1963; 1973). Elkonin (1963) trained children to segment spoken words by presenting them with a picture of an object under which there were little boxes for the number of sounds that made up the word. For example (in English), there might be a picture of a cat with three connected, empty boxes underneath it. The child's task would be to say each sound in *cat*, placing a token in each box as s/he did so. Children would be trained to eventually perform phonemic segmentation and phonemic replacement ("word changing") on an intellectual plane, without even having to say the stimulus word aloud. Elkonin (1973) presented little data for the effectiveness of his phonemic analysis training method although he claimed that "It [training] was followed by improvements in various aspects of learning literacy" (p. 569). Although it is not clear whether or not this training program facilitated the acquisition of reading skill ("learning literacy"?), perhaps it can be assumed that such training was successful in its own right. At present, there are other research reports that support Elkonin's basic contention that such skills can be trained.

Marsh and Mineo (1977) gave their four- and five-year-old prereading subjects training over four days on a forced-choice matching-to-sample procedure. A taped voice asked subjects to indicate which word began (or ended) with a given sound. Marsh and Mineo also varied whether or not a grapheme visual cue was present and counterbalanced whether the phoneme in question was a stop consonant, e.g., *d*, or a continuant, eg., *s*. In the four transfer sessions the visual cue was removed and phoneme types switched.

Their results, although not related to reading achievement, are of theoretical importance for reading. First, they showed that children can be trained to recognize phonemes, because performance significantly improved over training days. Second, one of the reasons often given for why segmenting phonemic units is difficult for children is that many phonemes sound different in isolation than in context. If this is true, then continuants that *can* be produced in isolation should be easier than stop consonants. When stop consonants are pronounced in isolation, the production of an extra *schwa* sound is unavoidable, e.g., *buh* for *b*. Marsh and Mineo found that continuants were significantly easier to recognize than stop consonants, regardless of their position in the word. Third, Marsh and Mineo created different allophones by sometimes releasing stops in the terminal position and sometimes not releasing them. If prereaders treat allophones as two different sounds, as some authors (e.g., Read, 1971) have found, then this would be an additional complication for the task of phonemic analysis. However, results indicated that children classed allophones phonemically rather than phonetically because there was no significant difference between allophone types.

What impact, if any, does this training in phonemic analysis have on reading achievement? Rosner (1971) used the Auditory Analysis portion of his Perceptual Skills Curriculum (1969) to train first graders who were judged by their teachers to lack reading readiness skills. He set up three groups: 1) a group of children who could read but did not get segmentation training (they had begun reading instruction in kindergarten because they had been judged to be "ready"); 2) a randomly-selected nonreading experimental group who received the segmentation training; and 3) a nonreading control group (also randomly selected) who did not receive training.

Apparently, Rosner's program was designed to move a child through a series of graded segmentation skills using first word-, then syllable-, and then phoneme-sized units. In fact, even before linguistic stimuli are used, the program uses music and hand clap segmentation tasks. Among the segmentation concepts this program teaches are (in order of presumed difficulty): that auditory information can be represented spatially first with dashes and then with writing; that these spatial representations can be "read"; that the presence or absence of auditory units can be recognized; that a missing auditory unit can be identified and produced; that elements can be deleted from auditory units and the remainder recombined; and that a segment in an auditory unit can be removed and replaced with another segment. Thus, the program trains phonemic analysis and synthesis skills and the concept that sounds can be represented spatially.

The training program was administered in 49 group training sessions for approximately 70 school days. In a pre-post test design, all children were given the Auditory Analysis Test (Rosner and Simon, 1971) prior to and after training. The two nonreading groups (experimental and control) had identical IQ and auditory analysis scores prior to training, and the reading group had significantly higher scores on both measures.

At the conclusion of the experimental group's training their scores on the Auditory Analysis Test were significantly higher than those of the control group, indicating again that auditory analysis skills can be trained. The control group's scores did not increase significantly despite the fact that all the children were being taught to read in first grade. The reading group's scores also improved significantly, although after the training the experimental group did not differ from the reading group on analysis skills. Because the reading group's scores improved it seems that reading instruction teaches additional auditory analysis concepts—at least to children who have some minimal analysis skills.

At the conclusion of training all children were given a reading test composed of 35 unit words taken from the instructional material and 25 "transfer" words not present in the instructional material. The experimental group was able to read significantly more words of both types than the control group. Although the reading group's scores were not given, Rosner reported that they remained ahead of the experimental group in reading. The fact that the experimental group read significantly more words correctly than the control group seems to be explained by their advanced analysis skills. Although these results suggest that the relationship between auditory analysis skills and reading achievement may be an important one, there is an experimental design problem in this and in the next study to be reviewed (Wallach and Wallach, 1976). In neither study did the control group receive supplemental training of any sort on reading or language materials. It is thus not possible to rule out experience with such materials as the cause of the effect.

Nonetheless, the Rosner (1971) findings on the effect of phonemic awareness training are impressive. Whether or not children required each of the many components of his program for as many as 49 sessions to demonstrate this effect is a question for further study. There may be some key exercises in this lengthy program that could do the job equally well. Also, Rosner did not report what type of reading instruction the children received. Presumably, reading instruction that emphasizes letter-sound relations would complement the impact of an auditory analysis training program more than a program concentrating relatively more on whole-word instruction. Bruce's (1964) study supports this contention: students from a school with letter-sound training had segmentation skills in advance of students from a school with whole-word training.

Wallach and Wallach (1976) did not leave the reading method to chance in their study; they designed their own. Thus, it is difficult to isolate the effects of auditory analysis training per se. The Wallachs' book describes their position on prereading skills, the program they developed, and an evaluation of its effectiveness. They argued, as other theorists (e.g., Savin, 1972) have, that the fact that children from lower socioeconomic backgrounds often fail at reading can be attributed to the failure of the average reading program to explicitly teach phonemic segmentation skills. Their program is intended to be used by non-professionals from the child's own community in a one-to-one tutorial supplement to whatever reading method exists in the classroom. As Wallach and Wallach put it:

> The program has three parts. In Part I the child learns to recognize sounds at the start of words, learns to recognize the shapes of letters, and learns to connect these letter shapes with the sounds. In Part II the child gains skill at recognizing and manipulating the sounds in any position in a word, including their blending, by work with the sounds and letters in short, regularly spelled words. Part III utilizes the child's regular classroom reading materials, adapting itself to whatever reading fare the teacher may be using (1976:78).

Wallach and Wallach selected first grade children scoring below the fortieth percentile on the Metropolitan Reading Readiness Tests. Half of these children then received the Wallach tutoring program and half did not. An example of some training steps are: decide whether or not a picture's name starts with a given sound; recognize the name of a picture after the tutor has said its name segmented into phonemes; build words with letters and sound them out; etc.

The impact of training on these phonemic segmentation skills was positive. When given the Spache Consonant Sounds Test, specifically the sections that assess knowledge of the starting sounds of words, the tutored subjects performed significantly better than the control subjects. With regard to the training's impact on reading, the tutored group exceeded the control group on a variety of measures: 1) on reading classroom text vocabularies; 2) on the standardized Spache word recognition lists; and 3) on the Spache reading comprehension test. In addition, by the end of the school year, the tutored subjects received higher grades in reading on their report cards than the controls. The discriminant validity data indicated that a general halo effect was not operating because the tutored group was identical to the control group on grades for mathematical skills.

The main problem with the Wallachs' study, however, is that it is difficult to disentangle the effects of phonemic awareness training from the effects of reading training. Clearly, the Wallachs seem to be demonstrating impressive gains with children who have poor prognoses for acquiring reading skill—witness the matched control group. However it is difficult to localize the source of the effect.

In conclusion, phonemic awareness skills—both analysis and synthesis—have been shown in a number of studies to be predictive of early and extended reading achievement. In fact, some studies suggest that phonemic analysis skills may be necessary for success with early reading instruction. For the child who may not have naturally acquired such skills (and why this might happen is an interesting, unexplained question in its own right), the literature suggests that their reading skills may suffer. However, with appropriate intervention in the form of some type of auditory analysis training, these children can apparently be helped. The literature contains many examples of successful attempts to train various segmentation and synthesis skills. In addition, there is evidence that reading instruction itself may indirectly train children in these analysis skills. However, in order to acquire these concepts through reading instruction a certain minimum level of such skills must already be possessed. The literature is unclear about what this minimal skill level must be. However, social class membership may predict who has phonemic awareness skills and who does not. Middle-class children who already have some phonemic awareness can be expected to develop the rest for themselves. Lower-class children who tend to have less of this awareness than middle-class children will more likely require instruction in these concepts.

If a child has received some type of phonemic awareness training, the literature indicates that the child's reading achievement is likely to be boosted significantly above where it would have been without the training. Thus, the data that have accumulated on the role of phonemic awareness skills in learning to read indicate that researchers who have selected these skills for study have been rewarded. They are skills that seem to bear a clear relationship to the reading skill, unlike other skills (e.g., cross-modal matching) that psychologists have chosen for study.

One of the most pressing additional research questions is whether or not auditory analysis skills can be used as a remedial device with a child who has already begun to fail in reading or with the adult nonreader (see Sticht, this volume). This is not to say that all reading failure can be ascribed to low level development of phonemic analysis skills; there are surely other causes (see Golinkoff, 1976). But it would be worthwhile to see if poor readers can be found for whom phonemic analysis is a problem. There is also a need to explore the long-term effects of phonemic awareness training programs. If the gains evinced are not long-lasting—even as they affect decoding skills alone—then auditory awareness skills will look less critical to the acquisition of reading skill than they presently do. Also, what are the entry skills of the children for whom these training programs will work?

In short, many unanswered questions remain. But evidence has accumulated that at least one type of prereading skill—phonemic awareness—seems to bear a critical relationship to the acquisition of reading skill. It is also clear that a child's failure to possess phonemic awareness skills can usually be remediated through training. Thus, the alphabetic principle upon which English orthography is based does not have to be abandoned and replaced by a syllabary (Gleitman and Rozin, 1973) for the purposes of initial reading instruction.

REFERENCES

Bruce, D. J. 1964. An analysis of word sounds by young children. British Journal of Educational Psychology 34:158–170.

Calfee, R. C. 1972. Diagnostic evaluation of visual, auditory, and general language factors in pre-readers. Paper presented at the American Psychological Association Meeting, September, Hawaii.

Calfee, R. C. 1977. Assessment of independent reading skills. In A. S. Reber and D. Scarborough (eds.), Towards a Theory of Reading. New York: Halsted Press.

Calfee, R. C., Chapman, R., and Venezky, R. 1972. How a child needs to think to learn to read. In L. W. Gregg (ed.), Cognition in Learning and Memory. New York: John Wiley & Sons.

Calfee, R. C., Lindamood, P., and Lindamood, C. 1973. Acoustic-phonetic skills and reading—kindergarten through twelfth grade. Journal of Educational Psychology 64:293–298.

Deutsch, C. P. 1964. Auditory discrimination and learning: Social factors. Merrill-Palmer Quarterly 10:277–296.

Elkonin, D. B. 1963. The psychology of mastering the elements of reading. In B. Simon (ed.), Educational Psychology in the USSR. Stanford, Ca.: Stanford University Press.

Elkonin, D. B. 1973. USSR. In J. Downing (ed.), Comparative Reading. New York: Macmillan.

Flavell, J. 1977. Cognitive Development. New Jersey: Prentice-Hall.

Fowler, C. A., Liberman, I. Y., and Shankweiler, D. 1977. On interpreting the error pattern in beginning reading. Language and Speech 20:162–173.

Fox, B., and Routh, D. K. 1975. Analyzing spoken language into words, syllables, and phonemes: a developmental study. Journal of Psycholinguistic Research 4:331–342.

Fox, B., and Routh, D. K. 1976. Phonemic analysis and synthesis as word attack skills. Journal of Educational Psychology 68:70–74.

Gibson, E. J. 1969. Principles of Perceptual Learning and Development. New York: Appleton-Century-Crofts.

Gibson, E. J. 1970. The ontogeny of reading. American Psychologist 25:136–143.

Gibson, E. J., and Levin, H. 1975. The Psychology of Reading. Cambridge, Mass.: M.I.T. Press.

Gleitman, L. R., and Rozin, P. 1973. Teaching reading by use of a syllabary. Reading Research Quarterly 8:447–483.

Gleitman, L. R., and Rozin, P. 1977. The structure and acquisition of reading. I: Relations between orthographies and the structure of language. In A. S. Reber and D. L. Scarborough (eds.), Toward a Psychology of Reading. New York: Halsted Press.

Goldstein, D. M. 1976. Cognitive-linguistic functioning and learning to read in preschoolers. Journal of Educational Psychology 68:680–688.

Golinkoff, R. M. 1976. A comparison of reading comprehension processes in good and poor comprehenders. Reading Research Quarterly 4:623–659.

Holden, M. H., and MacGinitie, W. H. 1972. Children's conceptions of word boundaries in speech and print. Journal of Educational Psychology 63:551–557.

Jeffrey, W. E., and Samuels, S. J. 1967. Effect of method of reading training on initial learning and transfer. Journal of Verbal Learning and Verbal Behavior 6:354–358.

Jenkins, J. R., Bausell, R. B., and Jenkins, L. M. 1972. Comparisons of letter-name and letter-sound training as transfer variables. American Educational Research Journal 9:75–86.

Liberman, A. M., Cooper, F. S., Shankweiler, D. P., and Studdert-Kennedy, M. 1967. Perception of the speech code. Psychological Review 74:431–461.

Liberman, I. Y. 1973. Segmentation of the spoken word and reading acquisition. Paper presented at the Society for Research in Child Development Meetings, Philadelphia.

Liberman, I. Y., Shankweiler, D., Fischer, F. W., and Carter, C. 1974. Explicit syllable and phoneme segmentation in the young child. Journal of Experimental Child Psychology 18:201–212.

Lindamood, C. H., and Lindamood, P. C. 1971. Lindamood Auditory Conceptualization Test. Boston: Teaching Resources Corporation.

Marsh, G., and Mineo, R. J. 1977. Training preschool children to recognize phonemes in words. Journal of Educational Psychology 69:748–753.

Muller, D. 1972–1973. Phonic blending and transfer of letter training to word reading in children. Journal of Reading Behavior 5:212–217.

Read, C. 1971. Preschool children's knowledge of English phonology. Harvard Research Quarterly 41:1–34.

Rosner, J. 1969. The Design of an Individualized Perceptual Skills Curriculum. Pittsburgh: University of Pittsburgh, Learning Research and Development Center Publication Series, #53.

Rosner, J. 1971. Phonic Analysis Training and Beginning Reading Skills. Pittsburgh: University of Pittsburgh, Learning Research and Development Center Publication Series, #19.

Rosner, J., and Simon, D. P. 1971. The Auditory Analysis Test: An initial report. Journal of Learning Disabilities 4:384–392.

Rozin, P., and Gleitman, L. R. 1977. The structure and acquisition of reading. II: The reading process and the acquisition of the alphabetic principle. In A. S. Reber and D. L. Scarborough (eds.), Toward a Psychology of Reading. New York: Halsted Press.

Savin, H. B. 1972. What the child knows about speech when he starts to learn to read. In J. F. Kavanagh and I. G. Mattingly (eds.), Language by Ear and by Eye. Cambridge, Mass.: M.I.T. Press.

Venezky, R. L. 1976. Prerequisites for learning to read. In J. H. Levin and V. Allen (eds.), Cognitive Learning in Children. Madison: University of Wisconsin Press.

Venezky, R. L., Green, M., and Leslie, R. 1975. Evaluation Studies of the Pre-Reading Skills Program. Technical Report #311. Wisconsin: Wisconsin Research and Development Center for Cognitive Learning.

Wallach, L., Wallach, M. A., Dozier, M. G., and Kaplan, N. W. 1977. Poor children learning to read do not have trouble with auditory discrimination but do have trouble with phoneme recognition. Journal of Educational Psychology 69:36–39.

Wallach, M. A., and Wallach, L. 1976. Teaching All Children to Read. Chicago: University of Chicago Press.

READING AS THINKING:
A Developmental Perspective

Hans G. Furth

Too often reading is presented in isolation from knowledge of language, which in the natural turn of events reading presupposes. Similarly, language is often treated without the obligatory constant recourse to human intelligence from which follows general knowledge and understanding. In this paper an attempt is made to clarify the place of reading within Piaget's theoretical framework of the development of intelligence. It is here assumed that for young children of primary school age the content provided by reading is not a suitable input to challenge their highest levels of intelligence. Such a challenging experience is "high-level" thinking, which is proposed as the immediate occasion that leads to intellectual growth. As a consequence, reading for young children is usually quite far removed from intellectual growth. If reading is presented as a performance that must be reached, as an achievement of great importance, the children will not experience school as a place where their growing intelligence is respected and fostered. This unfortunate situation can be characterized as "the thinking-reading gap"—children know more than they can verbalize in spoken or written language. It is a serious dilemma for any teacher of primary school children.

There is, however, another side to this dilemma that suggests not merely the possibility of treating aspects of reading as high-level thinking but also provides a solid foundation for the avoidance of premature reading failures and for success in intelligent reading. This other positive point of the paper is presented by the concept of a School for Thinking for children between 5 and 7-years of age, the age when traditionally the first formal instruction in reading begins. A School for Thinking is of course much more than a setting where children are exposed to reading. Indeed, reading is here treated more like a by-product of an overall thinking atmosphere where one will find many activities with only very indirect connections with reading. This follows from the first point of the argument that high-level thinking is much broader than and usually quite unrelated to language and reading. But at the same time that general developmental acquisitions are being fostered, the children of necessity will acquire what can be termed the psychological prerequisites of reading. They will acquire these not as boring exercises done for the sake of reading—a goal that is not motivating by itself—but as self-motivating thinking activities. In this manner the acquisition of reading will take place within an atmosphere of high-level thinking and the children will have the healthy opportunity to understand experientially the connection between reading and language and thinking that is treated below in a theoretical manner.

The psychological process of reading must therefore be understood within the framework of a person who knows the spoken language of a society. In turn, language is one among other manifestations of the symbolic capacity that makes symbolic communication, such as language, possible. Finally, all these processes, reading and language and symbolic representations, have their source in an intelligence that is common to and characteristic of all human beings. The relation of reading and thinking is therefore a close one. This relation should be regarded as asymmetrical insofar as we hold that thinking without reading, indeed, without language, is quite possible, although the reverse is not the case: there can be no linguistic behavior and hence no reading without some level of thinking underlying the linguistic act.

The word *thinking* can be illustrated more fully by a focus on the concept of human intelligence and by a description of it, not in terms of intelligence tests, but as the sum total of available cognitive structures. These structures organize all practical and theoretical behavior. Thinking can then be said to be the active application of theoretical intelligence; in other words, intelligence is regarded as the capacity and thinking is its actual application. However, this description does not suffice because there are different levels of thinking. It is really quite impossible to use scientifically any psychological term of everyday language without specifying its precise meaning and limiting its extension. Therefore, the following condition is added to the meaning of thinking as used here, after it is recalled that the extension of thinking is already limited to theoretical rather than practical intelligence: the application of *practical* intelligence in a goal-directed practical action is called intelligent action but not necessarily thinking; thinking is the application of *theoretical* intelligence, that is, an intelligence that can separate self, action, and object. Theoretical intelligence is not the same as formal intelligence: it includes all intelligence that develops beyond the sensorimotor stage and is ushered in around age 2 by what Piaget calls the construction of the permanent object, the first glimmer of theoretical intelligence.

The capacity to treat objects theoretically makes it possible to treat them symbolically, and as a consequence the functional constraints of external reality do not automatically impose themselves on the person who uses symbolic representations. Therefore those activities, whether symbolic or not, that are not directed toward a logically consistent understanding shall be excluded from the meaning of thinking. In other words, thinking is understood as some form of logical thinking as opposed to such human activities as daydreaming, fantasying, or even creative expressions. So our definition of thinking is: The application of theoretical intelligence in order to understand an event in a logically consistent and adequate manner.

Why are all these conditions added? Because apart from different *types* of thinking, there are different *levels* of logical thinking, and because there are no rigid criteria that allow a categorical statement that one level of understanding is thinking and another is not. If as a reader you understand the two previous sentences, you will appreciate that one person may understand them better or worse than another and that a criterion below which we would declare that the sentences were not read with adequate thinking will always remain somewhat arbitrary and relative.

Nevertheless, as this example shows, several levels of thinking or understanding can be distinguished: take a person who does not know the English language but knows how to decode, that is, pronounce the written language correctly or a child who knows English and can decode the sentences but is incapable of understanding their meaning, or finally adult readers of the English language who understand sentences in various degrees. Neither the first nor the second examples demonstrate reading in an adequate manner, although they exemplify important, perhaps even the most important *material* aspects of reading. Crucial to the discussion is the claim that some level of thinking is present in all examples of reading, including those that were called material reading, that is, reading apart from understanding. Decoding by itself is a thinking activity, even though it may not be reading. One major argument of this chapter is that this decoding activity is partly based on the proper development of cognitive structures related to listening and looking. These structures are products of theoretical intelligence and not simply the learning and memorizing of a given number of sight-sound connections.

But there is another, equally important, argument that is also based on developmental considerations and the *thinking-reading gap*. To understand this expression, the concepts of high-level and low-level thinking are essential. It has been mentioned several times that human intelligence can be applied to the understanding of given events at different levels. This statement implies not only individual differences between persons, but above all differences in the way a person functions. Depending on a variety of circumstances, individuals of all ages will apply their available cognitive structures in an uneven manner, sometimes in a better, sometimes in a worse manner. Although this is true of all persons, it must be remembered that particularly in the case of children the picture of a given, available intelligence is quite misleading. In children intelligence is above all a developing capacity that constantly tends to go beyond itself, so that for a child to be alive is synonymous with the child's intelligence growing and expanding beyond the present state. It is probably not possible to pinpoint the precise causes or occasions that bring about the gradual restructuring of cognitive structures, but it would seem reasonable to assume that intellectual growth takes place when children use their intelligence at a high level relative to their own habitual functioning, rather than at a low or routine level. Just as children acquire the skill of using their hands intelligently by handling objects in increasingly complex situations, so they acquire and expand their intelligence by using it at a high level. In short, high-level thinking is here postulated as the immediate occasion of intellectual development in all children and if the term high-level thinking is still too technical, the phrase, "challenging intellectual experience," can be used as long as it is clear that the experience must challenge a child's

most advanced cognitive structures. Note that what is construc-
tively challenging to one child may be to another child either too
low and hence not challenging or too high and hence lead to
intellectually unhealthy misconstruction and deformation.

The thinking-reading gap points out the dilemma in which a
school system finds itself when it places reading as one of the
main goals in the early primary school years. When Piaget set out
to observe the intellectual development of young children below
age 12 he quickly came to the conclusion that high-level thinking
is centered on action and in no way on language. Indeed, Piaget
states categorically that verbal thinking in pre-adolescence is
marginal to "real" thinking and does not attain the operatory
level of which the child is capable in action situations. Piaget
refers here to verbal representation as inappropriate occasions in
which to look for high-level thinking, and what is true of spoken
language is doubly true for reading and writing. To put the same
thought in simpler words: A child knows and understands more
than he or she can verbalize and to reach the highest or the
optimal level of thinking in any child below the age of formal
operations (beginning around 11 to 12 years) a primary focus on
language or reading is psychologically inappropriate and coun-
terproductive.

The sketch presented in Figure 1 is an attempt to illustrate
in a diagram the relation of language and reading to intelligence.
Intelligence is here conceived developmentally as cognitive
structures that regulate contact between a person and events and
establish the subject-object relation that constitutes the knowing
and understanding of an event. The upper part pictures a person's general intelligence and the two lower parts are restricted
to the general knowledge peculiar to competence in spoken language and in reading of that language, respectively.

The diagram in its upper part indicates that cognitive structures by which a person assimilates a present event (arrow from
the event to the structure) and accommodates to the event (arrow
from the structure to the event) constitute the basic instruments
for knowing and understanding, whether as structures of practical intelligence (PS) or of theoretical intelligence (TS). Cognitive
structures are constructed by feedback from the person's activity
of assimilation and accommodation; in other words, intelligence
grows by the active use of intelligence. (This developmental
feedback or developmental experience is shown by the thick

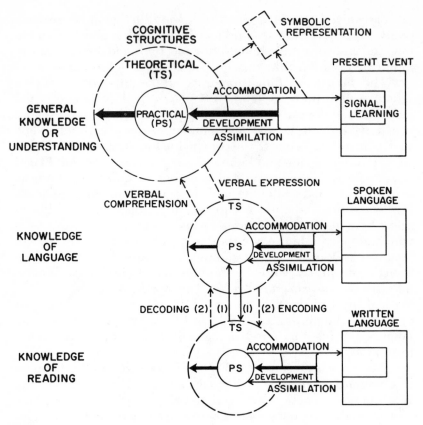

Figure 1.

arrows.) Developmental feedback is also responsible for the progression from practical to theoretical intelligence and this theoretical intelligence is the basis for the formation of symbols, including language, as shown by the two broken arrows that lead to symbolic representation. One of the arrows indicates the meaning aspect of a representation—its link with theoretical structures—and the other the material aspect of a representation—its link with aspects of the environment to which the structures accommodate. The material aspect provides the medium or the modality of a representation, such as gestural-motor, visual, auditory, or verbal material. The diagram shows as part of the known event an area called "signal" by which a particular event is identified and subsequently recognized. Signals are related to particular environmental content and to *learning* in the strict sense of taking in specific environmental information. In contrast, *development* is the progressive construction of general cognitive structures that derive not from the environment—as does the content of learning—but from the activity of the person. From the diagram it can be seen that learning is more closely related to the outgoing accommodative aspect of knowing, and development is more related to the inner-directed assimilative aspect. Moreover, developmental feedback that expands theoretical structures is identical with what was earlier called high-level thinking.

The two lower parts of the diagram illustrate the peculiar knowledge underlying the use of spoken language and of reading. Similar psychological processes to those discussed above take place, except that they are specifically geared to the particular medium of understanding speech and reading respectively. The practical structures (PS) refer to the material aspects of listening and articulating for speech and of looking for reading. The theoretical structures (TS) refer to the meaning aspects of language. These structures could be called linguistic competence—the state of being "at home" in a certain language—while the corresponding reading competence is more tentatively described as visual strategies that support meaningful reading, such as knowing what a word, a sentence, or a paragraph looks like, or even what an English word—as distinguished from a nonsense or foreign word—looks like. The developmental feedback peculiar to linguistic and reading behavior, shown by the thick arrows, is primarily responsible for the development of linguistic and reading competence, to a greater extent than the accommodative aspect connected with the learning of specific environmentally given configurations. This is probably what Chomsky and his associates refer to as the "innateness" of linguistic knowledge as opposed to the learning and memorizing of specific connections. Nevertheless, as indicated by the accommodation arrows leading to specific speech or reading situations, the process of learning in the strict sense is certainly obligatory in the acquisition of speech or reading—just as it is in the construction of general intelligence—but it must be seen as subordinate to the developmental acquisition of general cognitive structures.

How is speech knowledge related to general knowledge? Linguistic knowledge does not exist by itself but derives functional meaning—as do all symbolic representations—by its connection with the general cognitive structures. Following the diagram and starting with a particular speech event—say, the sentence "Dinner is going to be ready quite soon"—this sound sequence is first assimilated to the hearing structures of the person and then to the linguistic knowledge by which it is understood as an English sentence with a particular grammatical structure, and finally it must be assimilated to the general knowledge and understanding of what this sentence means—this is indicated by the broken arrow labeled verbal comprehension. It should be obvious that the knowledge of what it means "to expect dinner soon" derives from present or past events that have basically nothing to do with language. Thus the understanding of language has its roots in general knowledge and not vice versa. A speech act in turn could be indicated by a reverse progression from recognizing and understanding a present event by means of general theoretical structures to the formation of a symbolic representation of this understanding in the verbal medium—see the broken arrow of verbal expression from general knowledge to linguistic knowledge issuing in a speech act.

Reading is related to general knowledge via linguistic knowledge and the two possibilities of linking reading and language are indicated by two pairs of arrows. One pair is labeled Decoding 1 and Encoding 1, and is relevant for the beginning reader or writer. Here the visual reading material is first connected with practical structures of language, that is, knowledge of the written material is connected to knowledge of the sound aspects of language. This is traditional sight-sound correspondence and constitutes in my opinion the fundamental aspect of what is specific in learning to read. However, for the advanced reader there is no need to go from sight to sound; rather, the reader habitually bypasses the sound translation and goes directly from reading knowledge to linguistic knowledge. This connection is shown in the diagram by the pair of broken arrows labeled Decoding 2 from reading to language and Encoding 2, in the case of writing, from language to reading.

Within this developmental framework, which will be recognized as being closely modeled after Piaget, the two arguments related to reading and its acquisition shall now be discussed in greater detail: first, that the more important components of reading competence are developmental acquisitions and should be treated as such rather than as things to be copied, learned, and memorized from outside instructions; and second, that high-level challenging thinking is occasioned by contact with present events and until the age of formal reasoning is far removed from language and even more from reading.

The entire field of analyzing the sounds of a spoken sentence, such as the identification and recognition of words, of stress patterns, of the sequential arrangement of phonemes, of the phonemes themselves, all these things are fundamental to reading and provide an apt example of development acquisitions. The phoneme /b/ in the three words *Bat, cupboard,* and *rob* is not one isolated element readily perceivable, but psychologically and acoustically corresponds to three different speech processes. A speech spectrogram would in fact show three different patterns with no clear boundaries between phonemes and no clearly recognizable characteristics of the same phoneme in the different words. If a child becomes capable of hearing the invariant phoneme /b/ in these three words, that is due to the child's interpretation and theoretical analysis of the sound configuration. This is a developmental skill of auditory thinking, not a piece of information that has been memorized. Showing the child who has not yet developed this auditory thinking the visual letter *b* and pointing out that it goes with the phoneme /b/ turns this potentially challenging auditory thinking task into a dreary memory task. As a consequence the child begins to attack the problem of reading in a psychologically inappropriate way—reading becomes a matter of memory instead of thinking—and moreover this attempt is bound to lead to repeated failure, insofar as the child is admonished to associate two things, one of which the child cannot grasp mentally. If, however, sound recognition were practiced as a thinking game for its own sake and without pressure for quick successful performance, then such a child would be in a position to acquire phoneme recognition as a self-motivating and developmentally interesting skill. In other words, auditory thinking relative to sounds, sequences, rhythm, pitch, etc., are appropriate activities for children entering school, but they should be presented as meaningful in their own right and not as mere prereading exercises. Only thus can teachers avoid scholastic failures, respect individual differences, and keep motivation high.

Take another example, namely the sequencing of visual elements, such as the recognition that *was* and *saw* are different sequences of the same letters. It is possible that a certain child may experience reading difficulties because of uncertainty in visual sequencing. When asked to practice such combinations, the child may find the assignment quite boring and more likely than not frustrating, because he or she is given to understand that this is a task to be learned and memorized rather than a task of thinking. It cannot be sufficiently stressed that all children, just as they enjoy living, enjoy high-level thinking. The proof for this assertion is found in every child alive who continues to grow in intelligence year by year and does so in spite of an educational system that does not encourage high-level thinking. Likewise it is obvious that cognitive structures are not things we memorize but rather things we are, like our own identity or other stable characteristics of our person. To hear three phonemes in *tub* and to distinguish this sequence from *but* for a person who has developed the appropriate cognitive structures of listening and looking, is not a task of memory but of applying theoretical structures towards the understanding of a given event, that is, *thinking* as defined at the beginning of this paper. If a child today has certain well-developed capacities of thinking, we know that this child went through a period when these capacities were in the process of acquisition and hence provided occasions for high-level thinking. In fact, I observed six-year-old children enjoy the occasion of playing a permutation game and to these children permutation was a meaningful, exciting concept although reading was still an unattainable and personally non-motivating goal.

So far one point of the argument has been demonstrated—important aspects of reading can be presented to the child as high-level thinking tasks and should be presented in this way in order to foster a thinking attitude toward reading and to avoid experiences of failure. It need only be added that these skills are dependent not only on well-developed behavioral capacities but frequently also on physiological maturation, over which the child has no conceivable control. If specialists in vision tell us that continuous near focusing (as required for reading) is a physiologically stressful activity for the human eye—which has evolved in the service of far vision—and that the visual system of some children as old as 6 or 7 years of age may not yet have matured adequately for near vision, it must be realized that any strict performance criterion of reading at age 6 or 7 can put an intolerable stress and an entirely unjustifiable burden on not a negligible number of children.

However, the variety of high-level thinking activities to which children of beginning school age should be exposed must not be limited to tasks that are potentially reading-related. On the contrary—and this is the other point of the argument—high-level thinking in children of primary school age and below is usually found in situations that have very little to do with oral, and even less with written, language. "Real" thinking, as Piaget puts it, is to be observed in events that the child can manipulate or act upon, events that are concretely given—hence the phrase "concrete operations." As an illustration, children can show a quite sophisticated understanding of various odds in probability games, of logical reasoning in symbol-picture logic, of visual perspective in transposition task, even of social and emotional situations in dramatic play acting, but none of these things could be accomplished simply by talking or reading about them.

This is not the place to report in detail the conception of a School for Thinking as outlined in Furth and Wachs (1974). In this book are described the activities that took place in a first- and second-grade classroom where the teachers attempted to put into practice what had first been proposed in Furth (1970). This classroom had children from severely disadvantaged backgrounds, but these children were given the clear message that each was a thinking person capable of performing a variety of challenging tasks; above all, capable of knowing and understanding something not because the teacher or the book said so and it was memorized accordingly, but because the child's intelligence—the cognitive structures that are developing within the child—provided the ultimate criterion. The characteristic of fully developed operations according to Piaget is reversibility and by this is meant that the cognitive structures have become stable and logically self-consistent; the person with these structures now has the power mentally to move within the cognitive framework and to understand and predict events accordingly. This is an exhilarating experience for any child who for the first time feels himself or herself the intellectual master of the situation. Logicians call this by the dry name of universal or necessary judgments, but if teachers call it thinking, children will understand this because it is very close to the core of their developing personality.

By way of conclusion, a primary school that wishes to provide an adequate overall environment for intellectual health must not put its main emphasis on reading because the verbal medium on its own is not conducive to optimal intellectual functioning until the age of formal thinking is reached, at around 11 to 13 years. Moreover, reading requires a particular degree of neurological and sensorial maturation as well as a particular motivation, both of which are frequently absent in children entering school. The proper age of reading acquisition, probably anywhere between 4½ and 8½ years, is not substantially related to the child's overall intellectual level. On the other hand, all children age 5 are fully within the period of a rapidly developing intelligence and they experience for the first time a new kind of thinking that is fully self-consistent and internally controlled in the form of concrete operations. If the primary school would focus on these challenging thinking situations and deemphasize accountability for formal reading—deemphasize, not necessarily eliminate—we would have a triple advantage of: 1) nourishing and furthering children's most important cognitive achievement, i.e., their intelligence; 2) avoiding experiences of failure and subsequent problems of motivation; and 3) preparing the children in the best possible way to become intelligent readers.

REFERENCES

Furth, H. J. 1970. Piaget for Teachers. Englewood Cliffs, N. J.: Prentice-Hall.

Furth, H. J., and Wachs, H. 1974. Thinking Goes to School: Piaget's' Theory in Practice. New York: Oxford University Press.

CRITIQUE:
Development of
Intellect and Reading

Frank B. Murray

The determination of the intellectual prerequisites for reading is confounded in part by the fact that reading and intelligence tests, particularly in the later years, share a core of common and closely related test items. In the early grades, correlations between non-reading intelligence measures and initial reading performance are dependably moderate and positive (Robeck and Wilson, 1974). The few children who acquire reading without school instruction are superior in intelligence, being nearly two standard deviations above the mean on the Binet tests. They have a mental age of 4.5 years at the time they begin to read, thus incidentally refuting a common notion that reading acquisition depends upon the prior accomplishment of 6.5 years of mental age (Durkin, 1966).

This general picture of the relationship between reading and intellect continues to hold when the intelligence measures are based upon Piagetian theory. Briggs and Elkind (1973), for example, found that early readers, matched in traditional IQ, sex, and social class, showed more advanced levels of intellectual development on concrete operativity tasks (high-level thought in Furth's terms) than children who were not yet reading. The correlations between various operativity measures and reading average about 0.50 (see Waller, 1977; Murray, 1978a, for reviews of this literature). As one example, Almy, Chittenden, and Miller (1966) found that conservation correlated 0.49 and 0.53 with reading readiness and 0.39 and 0.37 with growth in reading for pupils in lower- and middle-class schools in New York City.

Surely these data confirm what no one ever doubted—that initial reading achievement and intellectual competence are related. Whether or not the relation is casual, and if so in which directions, remain unresolved theoretical and empirical questions (Ehri, 1978). The possibilities are the obvious ones, A causes B, B causes A, some third factor C causes both A and B; or, as is argued in this response to Furth's position, that the causal links between reading and intellect are reciprocal (Overton and Reese, 1973). The issue may be vitiated entirely by enlarging the meaning of reading to include all intellectual functions, as when reading is defined as thinking (Waller, 1977). Consider, for example, Guilford's (1967) structure of intellect (SI) model, consisting of 120 separate mental ability factors. Each of these is one of six products that result from the action of one of five mental operations on one of four contents (figural, syntactic, semantic, and behavioral). Although there is not a reading factor, decoding factor, or comprehension factor among these 120, a case can be made that all 120 factors support reading as it is conceived by one or another researcher. The figural, syntactic, and semantic contents in the SI model, for example, are the stimuli of all reading tasks, and if the behavioral context of the reading task is considered as part of the reading task stimuli then all of Guilford's SI contents are the stimuli of the reading task. The process of reading as it is described in various information-processing models (see Farnham-Diggory in this volume) employs all the SI operations (memory, cognition, convergent and divergent production, and evaluation). The various reading responses themselves can each be viewed as one of the SI products (units, classes, relations, systems, transformations, and implications). Reading can be conceived as the mental construction of classes, relations, systems, transformations, and implication products from print.

A similar case can be made for the functioning of the various mechanisms of the Piagetian model of operational intelligence in reading and its acquisition (Wadsworth, 1978). Furth's analysis of the relationship between reading and the development of intelligence in the previous chapter is unfortunately limited to a consideration of only the contributions intellect can make to the eventual development of the reading. His conclusion is that because language and reading always operate at a level below the highest level available in thought (we always know more than we can tell), the development of intelligence cannot be enhanced or promoted, especially in young children, through language and reading. Putting aside Croce's counterposition that unexpressable knowledge is not knowledge, the issue as Furth has drawn it can stand further examination. There is no question, as Furth acknowledges, that many of the features of operational thought, or theoretical intelligence as he calls it, can operate in the reading process itself—such as processing print from left to right and top to bottom (seriation), the recognition that words have spoken and written forms (decentration), the recognition of the relationship of the parts of a word to each other and to the whole word (class inclusion), the recognition and resolution of grapheme-phoneme correspondences (multiplication of classes and relations), or the recognition of form classes, function words, morphemes, and allomorphs (classification). Moreover, the child's appreciation of orthographic structure and the probabilistic sequences of language segments that undergird the decoding of new words have obvious links to operational thought. These speculations on the link between operational intelligence and reading are supported somewhat by a number of correlations that have been reported in the literature between initial reading performance and one or another of the various measures of operativity, namely conservation, seriation, transitivity, and classification (Fishbein and Emans, 1972; Waller, 1977; Murray, 1978a). Finally, the very Piagetian structures, hypothetical as they might be, that are alleged to support the comprehension of physical events and the universe in general would obviously be a part of the comprehension of prose passages that, if nothing else, are a part of the world (Stack and Murray, 1976).

The question is whether or not the relationship between thinking and language/reading is as asymmetrical as Furth claims it is. The issue hinges in part on finding a way in which the three kinds of events in Furth's figure, namely physical events, spoken language, and written language, differ and on whether or not the differences between these categories of stimuli are sufficiently great to require the complicated and hierarchically ordered differential processing the Furth figure indicates. Piaget is quite clear that the child constructs a mental structure of concepts out of a set of sensorimotor operations on categories of physical objects and events. It is a structure of consistent and necessary links between concepts. Out of the child's manipulation of a set of stones comes not only information about a stone's physical properties, but more importantly the knowledge that the number of stones has to be constant regardless of their various spatial arrangements. This kind of knowledge, which has little to do with the physics and chemistry of rocks, is the basis of intelligence as Piaget treats it.

Cannot similar contributions to intelligence be based upon

the manipulation of printed material? Are not the syntactic consistences of orthographic structure as real as the mathematical and physical consistencies that form the basis of the intellectual contributions Piaget and others have documented (cf. Gruber and Voneche, 1978)? Is not the construction of "letter" and "alphabet" as significant as the construction of "number"? It makes as much sense to speak of conservation of letter under transformations of case and font as it does number under transformations of spatial arrangement. The alphabet has cardinality and ordinality that are as consistent and necessary as those of a numerical system. The point is that written language is as lawful a system as any of the physical and mathematical systems and relationships that Piaget has claimed contribute to the development of intellect. It is reasonable to suppose that the child's consideration of written language will engage that high level of thinking that promotes cognitive growth in the same way his consideration of other events promotes this growth.

The benefit of the application of the operativity structures to written language would probably not accrue to reading proficiency as it would to the development of intelligence and to the child's understanding of the reading task itself. Children can play the thinking games Furth (1970) and Furth and Wachs (1974) advocate with written language stimuli. The permutation game, for example, can be played with letters rearranged in as many words as possible, or with words arranged in as many sentences as possible. That children do read proficiently without appreciating orthographic structure, etc., or without manifesting concrete operational thought only indicates that operativity is not necessary for reading although, as Furth argues, it may be sufficient for it. Indeed, such reading performance is not unlike the performance of children who count accurately but fail to conserve number. Furth is no doubt correct in arguing that the school's emphasis on reading performance does not promote thinking, particularly when the activity reaches a certain level of automaticity. At the same time, Furth should acknowledge that written language can be understood and reflected about in a way that "challenges intellectual experience," and that if it were taught from that perspective both reading and intellect would be enhanced. Instruction of that sort is a suitable objective for the grade school.

That the correlations between operativity and initial reading are not perfect means, of course, that some children read without manifesting operational thought. Such reading performance is presumably described by a model different from the one presented in Furth's diagram. The reading skill, like the rote use of the arithmetical algorithms, can be performed in a nonreflective way. What preoperational children think about the reading process is not known and studies of "meta-reading" would be instructive. Moreover, there is the attractive hypothesis that a reading mind is qualitatively different from a nonreading one, not so much because of the information it acquires this way as because of the process itself (Olson, 1976).

Nevertheless even nonreflective automatic reading proficiency may provide critical, even if vicarious, experience and information that contributes to intellectual development. Information acquired by reading as well as by actual conversation can promote the breakdown of the egocentric limitations of preoperational thought. Beilin (1978, in press) has reviewed a segment of the research literature that shows "how conservation can be acquired by linguistic means, despite Piaget's and Sinclair's assertions that conservation is not acquired in this fashion." There is virtually no doubt now that information contained in language can bring about genuine conservation in nonconservers (e.g., Murray, 1978b).

Finally, Furth's position that reading is a spontaneous by-product of high-level thinking is not consistent with the simple fact that there are cognitively mature adults, even in the Genevan sense, who do not read (see Sticht, this volume). Moreover, few people learn to read without the benefit of some systematic and protracted instruction and practice in decoding. The argument is hung inevitably upon the need for empirical data that demonstrate spontaneous positive transfer from high-level thinking to initial reading. Unfortunately such data have not been reported. The attempt to evaluate the implications of Piaget's account of intelligence for reading is made difficult because Piaget has no position on reading. The word *reading* does not even appear in the index of a recent work that Piaget describes as "the best and most complete of all the anthologies of my work" (Gruber and Voneche, 1978). In the end, the claim that there are high-level thinking prerequisites for reading cannot rest solely on the authority of Piaget. As it is, the data such as they are indicate that although operativity is not necessary for reading acquisition, it could be sufficient for it.

REFERENCES

Almy, M., Chittenden, E. and Miller, P. 1966. Young Children's Thinking. New York: Teachers College Press.
Beilin, H. 1978. Constructing cognitive operations linguistically. In H. Reese (ed.), Advances in Child Development and Behavior. New York: John Wiley & Sons, in press.
Briggs, C., and Elkind, D. 1973. Cognitive development in early readers. Developmental Psychology 9:279–280.
Durkin, D. 1966. Children Who Read Early. New York: Teachers College Press.
Ehri, L. C. 1978. Linguistic insight: threshold of reading acquisition. In G. Waller and W. MacKinnon (eds.), Reading Research: Advances in Theory and Practice, Vol. 1. New York: Academic Press.
Fishbein, J., and Emans, R. 1972. A Question of Competence: Learning, Language and Learning to Read. Chicago: SRA Associates.
Furth, H. J. 1970. Piaget for Teachers. Englewood Cliffs, N. J.: Prentice-Hall.
Furth, H. J., and Wachs, H. 1974. Piaget's Theory in Practice: Thinking Goes to School. New York: Oxford University Press.
Gruber, H. and Voneche, J. J. (eds.) 1978. The Essential Piaget: An Interpretive Reference and Guide. New York: Basic Books.
Guilford, J. P. 1967. The Nature of Human Intelligence. New York: McGraw-Hill Book Company.
Murray, F. B. 1978a. Implications of Piaget's theory for reading instruction. In S. J. Samuels (ed.), What Research has to Say about Reading Instruction. Newark, De.: International Reading Association.
Murray, F. B. 1978b. Teaching strategies and conservation training. In A. M. Lesgold, J. W. Pellegrino, S. Fokkema, and R. Glaser (eds.), Cognitive Psychology and Instruction, pp. 419–428. New York: Plenum.
Olson, D. 1976. Theory of instructional means. Educational Psychologist 12:14–35.
Overton, W., and Reese, H. 1973. Models of development: methodological implications. In J. Nesselroade and H. Reese (eds.) Life-Span Developmental Psychology. New York: Academic Press.
Robeck, M. C., and Wilson, J. 1974. Psychology of Reading. New York: John Wiley & Sons.
Stack, W., and Murray, F. B. 1976. Operativity and reading comprehension. Paper presented at the Sixth Annual Symposium of the Jean Piaget Society, June, Philadelphia.
Wadsworth, B. J. 1978. Piaget for the Classroom Teacher. New York: Longman.
Waller, T. G. 1977. Think first, read later! Piagetian prerequisites for reading. In F. B. Murray (ed.), IRA Series on the Development of the Reading Process, Newark, De.: International Reading Association.

HOW TO STUDY READING:
Some Information Processing Ways *

Sylvia Farnham-Diggory

Let us begin with a description of the stages—not those that children go through in learning to read, or that a reader goes through during the act of reading, but those that *psychologists* go through in learning how to study reading. These are the stages of Academic Psychological Reaction to the reading problem, or APR Stages for short. They characterize the development of very smart adult psychologists who have spent most of their professional lives in the laboratory, and who emerge from it rather suddenly when they discover how interesting reading behavior is.

APR STAGES I AND II

APR Stage I is the stage of complete confidence that within a few months the whole issue will be wrapped up. Reading problems are clearly an artifactual result of ignorance on the part of classroom teachers. Reading is obviously a collection of operations that laboratory psychologists know all about—short-term memory, attention, paired-associate learning, coding, and so forth. Once the teacher also understands these things, she will instantly see how to fix the reading pedagogy, and that will be that. Note the division of responsibility: the psychologist merely presents data. Putting them together and designing the pedagogy is someone else's problem.

   Stage I usually persists until the psychologist's first-born child (a son) enters first grade and fails to begin to learn how to read. At this point, the psychologist enters very abruptly into

* Prepared for the Second Delaware Symposium on Curriculum, Instruction, and Learning: The Acquisition of Reading, June, 1975. The preparation of this paper, and the research reported therein, was supported by Public Health Service Grant No. MH-07722, from the National Institute of Mental Health.

APR Stage II. This is the stage of fixing the reading pedagogy. At this time a large grant is obtained, and very complex arrangements are made with the local school system for training teachers, and for implementing the new pedagogy, and of course for evaluating it. Also at this time, the psychologist begins to attend educational meetings, gives talks on the One Correct Pedagogy that is now under construction, and becomes generally well known as an authority on reading. (It should be noted that there are also some linguists in this stage.)

Stage III comes on somewhat more gradually than Stage II did. Several things contribute to it. In the first place, evaluation is revealing that many children in the program do spectacularly well on the simple rote learning phases of the pedagogy (the data that were widely reported during APR Stage II) but fail to make a transition to more advanced phases of reading. The children, in effect, read their training materials just fine, but cannot generalize the rules in them—which is to say, they are not learning to read.

A second factor contributing to the onset of Stage III is that the psychologist himself has begun to read in the educational literature, and has met some very smart educators. And he discovers that his brilliant new pedagogy was, in fact, invented for the first time 250 years ago, has been reinvented several times since then, and was last discontinued as a published curriculum by Scott, Foresman & Company 5 years ago.

Most importantly, of course, the psychologist's son is still not learning how to read. What's worse, the psychologist's second-born child (a daughter) started to read spontaneously at the age of 3 without ever having been near any formal pedagogy. (If the psychologist is clinically inclined, this sometimes gives rise to a new phase of the pedagogy, called a Lap-Sitting Method of Reading Instruction—which will not be further pursued here.)

APR STAGE III

Stage III is the stage that most of us are in now. It is a very sober stage, characterized by an awareness of how arrogant and over-simplified our previous conceptions were. We realize, finally, that we cannot get from a simple paired-associates paradigm to the kind of reading behavior illustrated by the psychologist's three-year-old daughter. We realize, furthermore, that the process of receiving formal classroom instruction in reading may or

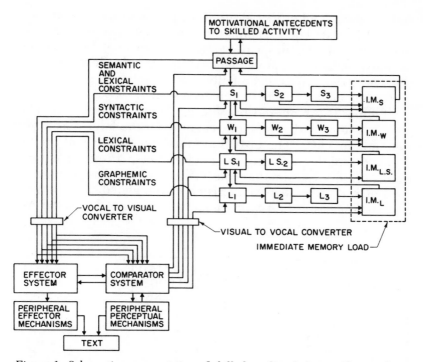

Figure 1. Schematic representation of skilled reading behavior (from Roberts and Lunzer, 1968: reprinted by permission).

may not be relevant to the process of productive reading itself. Now, at last, we begin to scan, scientifically, the full range of the problem.

Stage III actually has two parallel tracks. Most of us are in one or the other—which is why we are still in Stage III. The fourth and final stage, still ahead of all of us, will be the integration of the two tracks of Stage III. Let us consider them.

Track IIIA: The Theoretical Track

Much of the work in this track has been collated in the volume edited by Frederick Davis (1971), The Literature of Research in Reading with Emphasis on Models. In that book, there are many charts of the reading process. For example, Figure 1 shows the Roberts and Lunzer (1968) chart. The perceptual process begins at the lower left (TEXT). Then a comparator matches the perceived information to stores that include graphemic, lexical, syntactic, and semantic information. There is a visual-to-vocal converter, which implies that all of these memories are in some sort of vocal format. The immediate memory stack seems rather far removed from the input devices, so it may not be an input memory, but an integrative memory. Because the flow of control (shown by the arrows) eventually comes back to the text, this is probably an eye-movement guidance system.

Figure 2 was offered by Venezky and Calfee (1970). The process begins with a forward scanning for the largest manageable unit, or LMU. The LMU's are the largest units that can be chunked rapidly, and may be single letters, strings of letters, words, or phrases. Simultaneously, material that has previously been picked up by the scanner is being integrated. The integration process has a short-term memory "scratch pad." In the As-

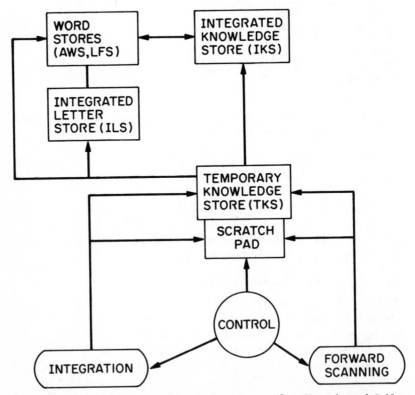

Figure 2. Schematic diagram of the reading process (from Venezky and Calfee, 1970: reprinted by permission of the International Reading Association).

sociative Word Store, there is a high frequency word store, where the retrieval process is based on minimal cues, such as initial letter or word length, and a low frequency store. Further affecting the integration process is the reader's knowledge of sentence types, of left-to-right rules, etc. And there is also an integrated *letter* knowledge store, which contains information on letter combinations.

Next, let us consider Jane Mackworth's model (1971), Figure 3. First of all, she distinguishes between a visual trace, or very short-term visual memory, and a longer-term visual memory. We

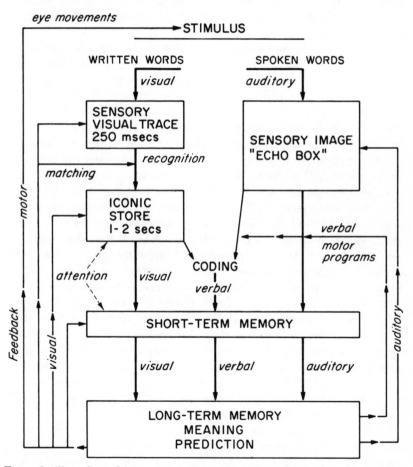

Figure 3. Flow chart of the reading process (from Mackworth, 1971: reprinted by permission).

can think of these as the Sperling memory, and the Posner memory, respectively. The Sperling image is gone in 250 msec, the Posner memory is gone in about 2000 msec.

The reason for postulating two visual memories is that we need to explain how the incoming visual information is held long enough to permit the development of complex auditory associations. Actually, we know from studies of visual recognition memory that there is a long-term visual memory as well, as indicated at the bottom of the Mackworth diagram. The figure also shows that there is a parallel auditory processing system. Apparently contact between the visual and auditory systems is made at the point of "coding." There are many feedback processes, even some that affect the visual trace.

Finally, in Figure 4, we have an example of quite a different type of model. This one has been developed by Rumelhart (1977), and utilizes some of the design features of a language-understanding computer program (Reddy and Newell, 1974). The problem in simulating language comprehension arises from the fact that many kinds of interpretation are going on simultaneously. The meaning or context of a statement influences interpretation; syntactical rules influence it, sound patterns influence it, and so forth. All of these interpretive processes interact with one another. Similarly, Rumelhart felt, many interpretive processes interact during reading. At the feature level, there are extraction processes. At the letter level, the results of the feature extraction process are analyzed, and hypotheses about letter identification are entertained. At a still higher level, the letter cluster level, the letter hypotheses themselves are scanned for known ortho-graphic regularities. The lexical level then postulates whole word possibilities. The syntactic level postulates word combinations. The semantic level evaluates the word combinations for sensibility. It is important to understand that processing at any level can occur whenever appropriate information is available. Thus, we could have semantic tests going on with respect to early parts of a sentence while feature tests go on with respect to later parts.

The above models are a sampling of work produced by individuals on Track IIIA, the theoretical track. The problem is, of course, how to evaluate these models. How can we tell if they describe, even in general terms, what actually goes on in the head of a reading person? Available data refer only to pieces of such models, and say nothing about changes that could result

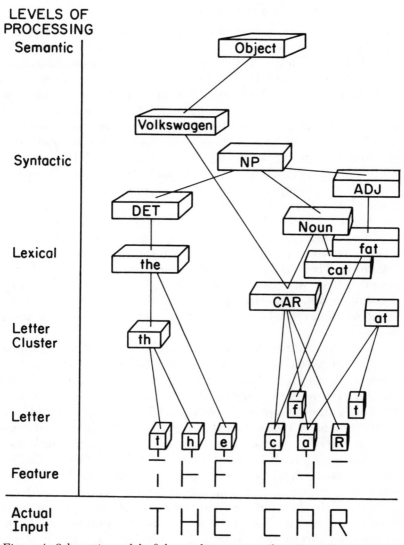

Figure 4. Schematic model of the reading process (from Rumelhart, 1977: reprinted by permission).

from interactions among pieces. Even more seriously, most of the data have been gathered with reference to no model at all.

Track IIIB: The Empirical Track

There are numerous ongoing research investigations of reading, and most of them are atheoretical. That is, most researchers believe that construction of a full-scale reading model is premature. More information needs to be gathered, they say, before any such elaborate theory could be put together. Some theoretical guidelines do exist, however; among them, the notion that reading involves visual activities and auditory activities. Reading also involves such processes as perceptual analysis, short-term and long-term retrieval, and strategies. The Track IIIB people, in other words, acknowledge that the Track IIIA people are dealing with the right components; but they are unwilling to get into the issue of how they all go together.

Quite a few Track IIIB people have hit upon the strategy of studying good and poor readers. The hope is that a particular reading component will not be working as well in the poor reading group. That would verify the importance of the component; it would tell us that such a component does in fact belong in a reading model. This strategy has the effect, however, of polarizing researchers who are pursuing a single cause of reading failure.

One pole houses researchers who believe that something is wrong with visual components. Kolers (1975) reported that poor readers are relatively poor letter pattern analyzers, where letter patterns are defined in terms of both normal and reversed type. The experimental question was whether subjects would correctly remember if they had seen a particular sentence in normal or in reversed type. Good readers were better at this task than poor readers were. Research by Stanley and Hall (1973a; 1973b) suggests that visual perseveration, rather than rapid fade-out, might be a source of the visual recognition deficit. In experimental tests of the first 300 msec of visual processing, poor readers displayed perseveration of the icon. This resulted in visual confusions and discrimination lags. Conceivably, initial discrimination difficulties could underlie the recognition memory difficulties reported by Kolers. (We will come back to the implications of perseveration for masking.) In yet another study of visual difficulties, Samuels and Anderson (1973) found that good readers were better than poor readers in recognizing Gibson letter-like forms that they had seen before.

A number of researchers, however, reject the notion that something is wrong with visual-analytical or memory abilities, and favor the likelihood that something is wrong with auditory or speech components of the reading task. Vellutino and his colleagues have been major supporters of this view (Vellutino, 1977). In a typical study, Vellutino et al. (1975) showed Hebrew letters to good and poor readers (of English) who were unfamiliar with the letter names. The poor readers displayed immediate and delayed recognition memories that were not substantially inferior to those of the good readers at fourth and sixth grade levels. There was a slight inferiority (of poor readers) at the second grade level. Both of these non-Hebrew speaking groups were outperformed by Hebrew-speaking groups, suggesting that knowledge of the letter names aided visual recognition of the letters. Many studies have provided data in support of hypotheses that phonetic or phonemic recoding skills are deficient in poor readers (Liberman et al., 1977; Rozin and Gleitman, 1977).

The modality researchers are generally not the same as the process or strategy researchers. The latter group addresses such questions as: How long does it take to retrieve the sound of a word, and does this speed vary with reading skill (Fredericksen, 1978)? Several investigators have been concerned with naming speed and rehearsal loops (Spring and Capps, 1974; Swanson, 1977; Torgesen and Goldman, 1977), forms of processing that are theoretically separable from modality. Spring and Capps (1974), for example, found that poor readers show recency but no primacy recall effects—a factor that was related to rehearsal strategies.

If modality and processing factors are orthogonal, then interactions can be anticipated. Lee Gregg and I investigated some of them (Farnham-Diggory and Gregg, 1975). The 24 fifth graders in the study were from a low socioeconomic area, from a school that has generated the lowest reading scores in the city. Many of the children were from Appalachian regions; a few were black. All of the children were tested individually in a session lasting about 45 minutes. They received 10 auditory memory span trials, 10 visual memory span trials (the stimuli were presented sequentially, as in the auditory condition), 40 auditory memory scanning trials, and 40 visual memory scanning trials.

The memory scanning questions were typical of those involved in the reading process—remembering which letter came first, which came last, and so forth.

The most important results of the experiment are shown in Figure 5. First of all, the buildup of proactive inhibition (PI) during the memory span trial was more severe in the group of poor readers, and did not dissipate in that group when modality

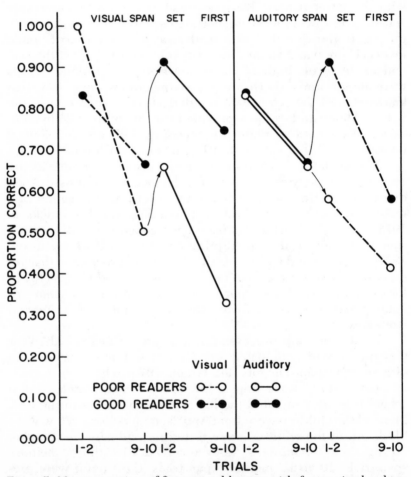

Figure 5. Mean proportions of first two and last two trials for ten visual and ten auditory span sets presented consecutively, showing differential proactive inhibition buildup and release for good and poor readers (from Farnham-Diggory and Gregg, 1975: reprinted by permission).

was switched. Among the good readers (filled circles) there was some PI buildup within each modality, but the experimental shift from either visual to auditory, or from auditory to visual modes of letter-set presentation produced a resurgence of correct responding—i.e., PI release. Among the poor readers, however, only slight release was produced by the visual to auditory switch, and no release was produced by the auditory to visual switch.

Figure 6 shows that a similar phenomenon characterized the memory scanning rates of the children. Over trials, the memory scanning speeds of good readers on auditory materials resembled their speeds to the same materials presented in the visual modality. Poor readers, however, developed an asynchrony of auditory and visual memory scanning speeds. One simple index of a developing asynchrony is the proportion of reaction time (RT) difference, between the auditory and visual functions, accounted for by the last 5 trials. In the good reading group, there was an overall difference of 28.6 sec in total RT to auditory materials, and total RT to visual materials. The last 5 trials accounted for 40% of this difference. In the poor reading group, there was an overall difference of 64.1 sec, and the last 5 trials accounted for 80% of it.

In the final analysis, the visual/auditory questions will probably require interhemispheric research paradigms. It seems clearly established by now that the hemispheres of the brain are specialized for different types of processing. Geffen, Bradshaw, and Nettelton (1972) and others have shown that name-matching in the standard Posner paradigm is faster in the left hemisphere, and that physical-matching is faster in the right hemisphere. Seamon and Gazzaniga (1973) extended this to mode of mediation: when subjects were instructed to use a verbal rehearsal strategy, a resulting matching response was faster in the left hemisphere; when subjects were instructed to use imagery mediators, the resulting matching response was faster in the right hemisphere. Cohen (1973) asked whether or not the left hemisphere was also specialized for serial processing, and found that it was—although it could do parallel processing if the task required it. The right hemisphere could not do serial processing very well. Miller and Turner (1973) showed there were some developmental effects in the lateralization of word recognition. It should be faster in the left hemisphere, and it was, but this effect becomes much more pronounced around the age of 9 or 10. These authors

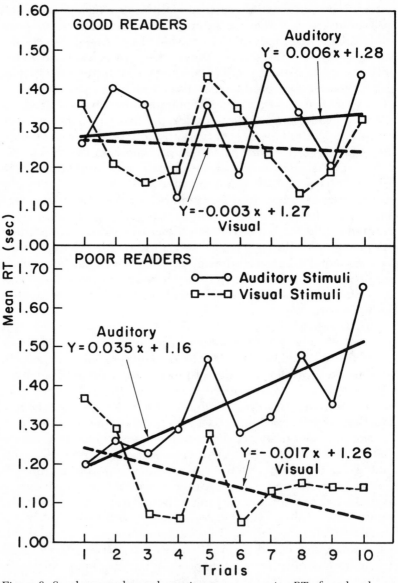

Figure 6. Synchrony and asynchrony in memory scanning RT of good and poor readers, over trials (from Farnham-Diggory and Gregg, 1975: reprinted by permission).

also found a correlation of about 0.60 of the degree of laterality with reading achievement. When age was partialed out, this dropped to 0.43, which was still highly significant in their sample.

The fact that hemispheric specialization in the brain exists tells us nothing, of course, about how these differential processing skills are managed. Much of the hemisphere management research has been done by Dimond and his colleagues (Dimond, 1971; Dimond and Beaumont, 1971; 1972a; 1972b). They use four projection screens, so that stimuli can be passed through the same eye to different hemispheres. Thus you can have factorial designs involving same eye vs. different eye, same hemisphere vs. different hemisphere, same word stimuli vs. different stimuli, and so forth. They have found, for example, that when the hemispheres compete, the right hemisphere reports more accurately than the left one does. One might infer, then, that poor interhemispheric management during reading might produce a situation in which the reader depends more than he should on the non-linguistic hemisphere, which might impair his reading. Another Dimond finding was that when competing words were passed through the same eye to different hemispheres, accuracy was poorer than when the competing words were passed through different eyes. The most damaging effect, however, was produced by passing competing words to the same hemisphere.

The research of Sandra Witelson (1976; 1977) and that of Davidoff, Cone, and Scully (1978) suggest that there is still a further dimension to the problem. In addition to the issues of hemispheric specialization and management, there is also the problem of functional integrity—some people's left hemispheres engage in right-hemispheric type processing, and vice versa. This may vary with age, and with reading ability.

To summarize thus far, there are many clues in the empirical literature to keep those of us in APR Stage III, Track B, hard at work. But the fact is that we must also work toward Stage IV—*the unification of empirical data with a detailed model of the reading process as a whole*. This should not imply that Stage IIIB researchers do not have theories. They often do, but they are very simple theories that are not adequate to the actual complexities of the reading process.

COMPONENTS OF STAGE IV

The field of information-processing psychology has developed three types of methodology that should help us construct more integrated formats for the study of reading.

First of all, there is the method of *protocol analysis*. At its most formal, this method requires us to match sequential data emitted by a subject to a theoretical simulation of the data. The theory, of course, specifies the components, mechanisms, and parameters responsible for the protocol. More informally, we can just pay attention to the details of subject output. For example, Table 1 contains some literal transcriptions of words that poor readers read aloud. Suppose we were to take these data quite literally as representing what these subjects thought they saw. The stimulus words in the left column were well-known to this group of fifth graders; they had practiced these words in their remedial reading classes. Nevertheless, when presented at a 2-second rate, the words were misread in these ways.

In some cases, letters seemed to be lost completely—as in "gree," "essmate," and "icomfort." In other cases, letters appear to have been displaced: "un*for*gridable" and "*sl*otion" may be examples. Note also how perseverating letters appear to have intruded into the integration process: "gi*lle*tte" and "a*tt*itude" are examples. And in many cases, common visual spelling patterns were misidentified: "re*ju*rious" instead of "re*ve*rence," "sol*ta*tion" instead of "solu*t*ion," "particu*las*" instead of "particu*lar*," "al*foon*ite" instead of "al*ter*nate." Note that many mis-

Table 1.   Examples of misreadings of three poor readers

| Test words | | Responses | |
	Subject A	Subject B	Subject C
screw	square	scree	gree
alternate	attitude	alfoonite	ellternate
companion	complete	compension	compension
definite	different	defynit	definite
estimate	instrument	extermate	essmate
majesty	maryjest	magjenate	majesty
glitter	gillette	glatter	groller
particular	particulas	presenter	parature
reverence	rejurious	revention	revensure
solution	solitude	slotion	soltation
uncomfortable	icomfort	uncomfortable	unforgridable

called auditory chunks were nevertheless valid chunks—
"*gla*tter," "solu*tude*," "instru*ment*" are well-practiced sound
patterns that did not happen to belong to the actual spelling
patterns in the test words.

The important point about these types of errors is that they
can also be produced in perfectly normal readers by manipulating the parameters of words presented on a scope. For example,
suppose 5-letter words are presented one letter at a time, with
each letter in its correct location, but out of order *temporally*
(Mayzner, Tresselt, and Cohen, 1966; Gregg, 1974). If the letters
come in very fast, so that the first letter is still "lit up" in the
Sperling memory when the last letter comes in—this would be at
about 60-80 msec total display time—then the word can be easily
read. If the letters come in very slowly, so that there is rehearsal
time for each letter—say, 400-500 msec total display time—then
the word can also be reported accurately, but this is really more a
matter of problem-solving than of reading off a memory image. If
an in-between display rate is used, say 200-300 msec of total
display time, then subjects report crazy words—very much like
these words reported by poor readers. This suggests, then, that
within the poor reader there are problems involving masking of
one letter by another—possibly because of a slower fade-out rate.
As the child looks at the word sequentially, the first part of it
should be out of his iconic buffer when the second part of it
comes in—otherwise there will be confusions and masking. Or
possibly there is a more central problem involving interhemispheric management. Information that has been picked up by the
right hemisphere may not get passed over to the left hemisphere
fast enough, for example. These possibilities are suggested only
to illustrate the potential value of carrying out a detailed theoretical analysis of the protocols of poor readers. If we assume they
are saying what they see, then what they are seeing must be
scrambled.

A second type of methodology developed by information
processing psychologists is the use of *converging data that fill in
a panorama of complex behavior.* Consider a task that may be in
certain respects the opposite of the reading task. In reading, the
graphemes go in, and the phonemes come out. In spelling, at
least in spelling from dictation—including self-dictation—the
phonemes go in, and the graphemes come out.

Imagine yourself writing the word *cantankerous*. Are you
going through the steps outlined in Figure 7? This description

1   generate sound frame

2   get next phonemic chunk

3   hold it in Working Memory

4   get an associated graphemic chunk
    and write it

5   does the written chunk match an item
    on the word recognition list (stored
    in the Language Generator)?

            if so, return to 2 (or 1)

            if not, return to 4

Figure 7.   Model of the spelling process (from Farnham-Diggory and Simon, 1975: reprinted by permission).

obviously oversimplifies the spelling task, but nevertheless, it is possible to gain some support for the validity of this little program by classifying errors into three types—sound frame errors, phoneme errors, and grapheme errors, as illustrated in Table 2 (Farnham-Diggory and Simon, 1976).

Each word in our error pool was classified as belonging to only one class of errors. If the sound frame was wrong, then phoneme and grapheme errors were not assessed. Phoneme errors were assessed only when sound frames were correct, and grapheme errors were assessed only when both sound frame and phonemes were correct. By *time* is meant the number of seconds spent writing a word.

Assuming a subject making an error is looping back through a particular level of his cognitive program, then sound frame errors should take a relatively long time to produce, because they occur at a deep level, while phoneme and grapheme errors occur at shallower levels, and should take less time, respectively. Table 3 shows that generally seemed to be the case.

Ordinarily in spelling, words are dictated or self-generated as sounds. For that reason the spelling program may be triggered

Table 2. Examples of sound frame errors, phoneme errors, and grapheme errors specified by the model in Figure 7

Correct word	Sound frame errors	Phoneme errors	Grapheme errors
October	Octberm	Atober	
rather	rathht	rater	
farmer	faere		farmmer
apple		appey	appel
dream	damer	dreen	driem

by word sounds. If so, and we *showed* children words that we wanted them to spell, rather than *said* them, their spelling should take a little longer, because of the sight-to-sound recoding step that would have to occur. We can call this *sight-spelling*. Table 4 shows that sight-spelling took a little longer in all cases.

Now we get to some interesting individual differences. All the children contributing the misspelled words used in the following analyses were disadvantaged—they lived in an urban ghetto, and attended the same integrated school. As shown in Figure 8, when we group their errors by modality of word presentation, we find that the increase in spelling time (or, rather, misspelling time) that follows visual word presentation is more characteristic of the white children than of the black children. Both meaningful words and nonsense words are represented here. The nonsense words were actually transpositions of the meaningful words—*merfar* was the nonsense transposition of *farmer*, for example. You can see that the black children generally spell more slowly than the white children do. They also make more errors, about 50% more on the average, but there could be a number of reasons for that—dialect reasons, for

Table 3. Mean number of seconds per word spelled correctly and incorrectly

	Mean seconds/word, incorrect spelling		
Mean seconds/word, correct spelling ($N = 633$)	Sound frame error ($N = 28$)	Phoneme error ($N = 91$)	Grapheme error ($N = 105$)
7.55	13.82	10.19	8.49

Table 4. Mean number of seconds per word spelled correctly or incorrectly, following visual exposure (sight-spelling) or auditory exposure (sound-spelling)

Exposure	Mean seconds/word, correct spelling	Mean seconds/word, incorrect spelling		
		Sound frame errors	Phoneme errors	Graphene errors
Sight-spelling	9.18 (N = 486)	17.6 (N = 25)	14.5 (N = 38)	10.0 (N = 24)
Sound-spelling	9.03 (N = 348)	15.3 (N = 30)	10.8 (N = 100)	9.4 (N = 95)

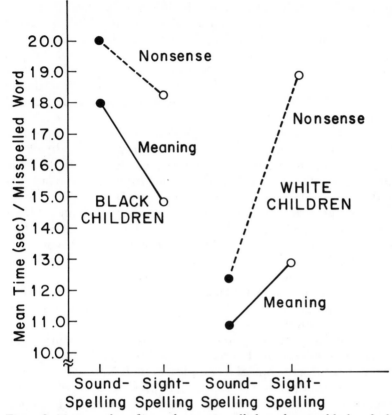

Figure 8. Mean number of seconds per misspelled word among black and white children.

example—and the difference in error rates is not important here. What is important is the difference in representational strategy suggested by differences in writing times when everyone was making errors, as they are here.

It can be seen that the white children always took longer when the word was visually presented, suggesting that they were recoding into a sound representation, and spelling from that. When the word was already in sound form, spelling was faster. However, the black children spelled faster from visual word presentation. Either they were not going through the same recoding steps as were the white children, or, alternatively, they were attempting to recode the sound of words into visual form when spelling from dictation. That could be why spelling from dictation is so extremely slow for black children, because it takes a long time to generate the visual image of a word. Why might that be a plausible thing to attempt? Consider the implication of dialect differences. If your teacher says a word one way, and you say it another, but it looks like the same word, you might be very well advised to try to remember what it looks like in order to spell it, because if you spell it the way it sounds to you, you will probably be wrong.

If black children do in fact rely more on a visual code than white children do, then we should be able to detect this by examining an aspect of spelling that is relatively independent of the sound factors. One example is the *visual frame* of the word, defined simply as the number of letters in it. If you spell a word wrong, but nevertheless rely on a visual code, you should at least get the number of letters in the word right, because that could be almost purely a matter of visual recognition memory. If you spell a word wrong, and do not rely on a visual code, then you should be less likely to preserve the correct visual frame.

Figure 9 shows that black children generally do have a higher percentage of correct visual frames than white children do—except when they are hearing a nonsense word, for which a visual frame is least likely to exist in recognition memory.

The immediate point is that several types of data were used here to paint in portions of a complex model. Note we were not using gross test data, but were trying to pick up facets of a single integrated program of behavior—facets concerning representation, sequential stages of the spelling process, meaning, and so forth. This is very different from administering a battery of tests that we think might index reading ability in some unspecified ways.

Finally, from the information processing world, we have *computer simulation methods.* A computer program that simulates the process of reading is probably the only type of model that will be adequate to the complexities of reading. To get from a flow chart like those shown in Figures 1, 2, 3, and 4, to the operating characteristics of a whole reader, we will need the kind of detail that can only be handled by a computer. Just as the oil refineries need to consider the complex interactions of variables like rate of flow, market shifts, monetary shifts, production rates, and so forth, so we need to represent ways in which a shifting panorama of variables interact to produce reading behavior.

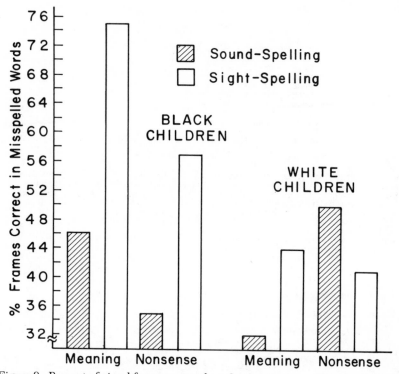

Figure 9. Percent of visual frames remembered correctly among black and white children.

Even more important than the representational power of the model, however, is the effect of the construction process on the ideas of the theorist. Figures 10a and 10b are samples of output by a program intended to simulate the decoding processes of an unskilled reader.[1] Some basic functions involved in the act of reading include the ability to detect a NEXT element, a SCAN-ing procedure, a SEARCH operation, and a BLENDing opera-tion.

The data stores, the long-term memory, consist of words and sounds that a ten-year-old subject would recognize. The symbol V1 here simply names a list of items where the first element denotes the visual input, and the second element denotes an associated phonemic pattern. This immediately brings up the interesting question of which visual input, and which phonemic

---

[1] The program was written in SNOBOL by my colleague Lee Gregg.

```
00050    -UNLIST
00100    *READING SIMULATION VERSION 8, 27 FEB, 1974
00200             &TRACE = 1000
00300         TRACE('VSTM','VALUE')
00400         TRACE('ASTM','VALUE')
00500         TRACE('REMEMBER','VALUE')
00800         INPUT('INPUT',2,80)
00900    *FUNCTION DEFINITIONS FOLLOW
01000         DEFINE('NEXT()')
01100         DEFINE('SCAN()')
01200         DEFINE('BLENDTEST()')
01300         DEFINE('SEARCH()')
01400         DEFINE('BLEND()')
01500         DEFINE('TEST()')
01600    *
01700    *MEMORY STRUCTURES CONSIST OF VISUAL AND AUDITORY DISCRIMINATION
01800    *NETS.  AN ITEM IN VISUAL STM IS SORTED TO A TERMINAL NODE
01900    *WHERE ASSOCIATED PHONEMIC DATA ARE POSSIBLY FOUND,  SIMILARLY
02000    *AUDITORY CUES FROM ATTEMPTS TO PRONOUNCE AND BLEND ARE
02100    *SORTED TO TERMINALS THAT CONTAIN VISUAL INFORMATION.  THE
02200    *VISUAL LONG TERM MEMORY NETS ARE DESIGNATED V1, V2, ,,,
02400    *
02500         V1 = 'P:PER;T:TA;C:SER;I:I;L:UL;LAR:LER;PART:PART;SI:SI;'
02600    *AUDITORY LONG TERM MEMORY NETS ARE
02700         A1 = 'PERTA:PART;ISER:SI;L:UL;ULLER:LER;'
02800    *
02900         VLTM = V1
03000         ALTM = A1
03100    *TOTAL MEMORY IS CONCATENATION OF VLTM AND ALTM
03200    *
03300    *FUNCTION DEFINITIONS
03400    *
03500         OUTPUT = 'START'          :(INIT)
03600    NEXT LOOK LEN(1) , VSTM                  :F(N1)
03700         NEXT = VSTM                         :(RETURN)
03800    N1   LOOK = WORD
03900         OUTPUT = 'EYE RETURNS TO BEGINNING OF WORD' :(NEXT)
04000    *
04100    SEARCH  VLTM VSTM ';' BREAK(';') , SAY        :(F(S1)
04200         ASTM = ASTM ' ' SAY
04300         SEARCH = SAY
04400         OUTPUT = ASTM                       :(RETURN)
04500    S1   OUTPUT = 'I DUNNO THAT LETTER'
04600         SEARCH =                            :(RETURN)
04700    *
04800    BLEND ASTM ' ' =                         :S(BLEND)
04900         OUTPUT = ASTM                       :(RETURN)
05000    *
05100    *VISUAL TEST OF SEGMENT AGAINST WORD
05200    TEST REMEMBER '-'                        :F(RETURN)
05300         MEMBER = REMEMBER
05350         REMEMBER =
05400         LOOK = WORD
05500         OUTPUT = 'LOOKS BACK TO CHECK WORD'
05600    TO   MEMBER '-'                          :F(RETURN)
05650         ASTM =
05700         MEMBER BREAK ('-'), ASTM '-' =      :F(T2)
05800         ALTM ASTM ':' BREAK(';') . VSTM              :F(T2)
05900         LOOK VSTM =                         :F(T2)
06000         ASTM =
06100         CHECK = SEARCH( )
```

Figure 10a. Sample of the SNOBOL program simulating the reading process.

```
06200                    CHECK ''                              :F(T1)S(T3)
06300        T1          OUTPUT = 'I THINK I AM RIGHT'
06340        T3          REMEMBER = REMEMBER ASTM '-'
06350                    SKIP = 'OK'
06380                    ASTM =                                : (TO)
06400        T2          OUTPUT = 'I AM IN TROUBLE'
06500                    ASTM =
06600                    VSTM =
06650                    REMEMBER =
06700                    LOOK =  WORD                          : (RETURN)
06800        *
06900        *
07000        BLENDTEST COUNT =
07100                    SAY = ASTM
07200        B1          SAY ' ' =                             :F(BL2)
07300                    COUNT = COUNT + 1                     : (B1)
07400        BL2         GT(COUNT,1)                           :S(B3)
07500                    BLENDER = 'NO'                        : (RETURN)
07600        B3          BLENDER = 'YES'                       : (RETURN)
07700        *
07800        SCAN PHONEME LEN(1) , LAST =                      :S(SCAN)
07900                    SCANNER =
08000        SC1         LOOK LEN(1) , NEW =                   :F(S2)
08100                    IDENT(NEW,LAST)                       :F(SC1)
08200                    OUTPUT = 'FIXATES THE ' NEW           : (RETURN)
08300        S2          OUTPUT = 'THE WORD IS ' REMEMBER ASTM
08350                    ASTM =
08400                    SCANNER = 'DONE'                      : (RETURN)
08500        *
08600        *
08700        *MAIN PROGRAM STARTS HERE
08800        *
08900        INIT OUTPUT = 'TYPE IN WORD YOU WANT ME TO PRONOUNCE'
09000                    WORD = TRIM(INPUT)
09100                    LOOK = WORD
09150                    SKIP =
09155        PO          REMEMBER '-'                          :F(PRONOUNCE)
09160                    MEMBER = REMEMBER
09165                    MEMBER BREAK('-') , ASTM '-' =        :F(PR2)
09170                    ALTM ASTM ';' BREAK(';') . VSTM       :F(PR2)
09175                    LOOK VSTM =                           :F(PR2)
09180                    ASTM =                                :F(PRONOUNCE)
09185        PR2         LOOK = WORD
09190                    REMEMBER =
09195        *
09200        PRONOUNCE LETTER = NEXT()
09300                    PHONEME = SEARCH()
09400                    SCAN()
09500                    SCANNER 'DONE'                        :S(EXIT)
09600                    BLENDTEST()
09700                    BLENDER  'YES'                        :F(PRONOUNCE)
09800                    BLEND()
09850                    SKIP 'OK'                             :S(P1)
09900                    REMEMBER = REMEMBER ASTM '-'
10000                    TEST()              : (PRONOUNCE)
10010        P1          ALTM ASTM ';' BREAK(';') . VSTM       :F(P2)
10020                    VLTM VSTM ';' BREAK(';') . ASTM
10030        P2          REMEMBER = REMEMBER ASTM '-'
10040                    ASTM =                                : (PO)
10100        EXIT                          : (PO)
```

Figure 10b. Sample of the reading simulation, continued.

pattern? Most studies of reading either assume, or tachistoscopically control, the size and nature of the visual input. But the protocols shown in Table 1 suggest that what is picked up is actually highly variable, at least in a poor reader. Similarly, there are a number of possible phonemic patterns that could be associated with any particular visual input. In our simulation, we did what is traditionally done experimentally—we chained particular visual-auditory elements. But a correct model should contain decision mechanisms for processing both the visual stimulus, and the storehouse of potential auditory associates.

The fundamental operations of the program involve the following subroutines. The computer first looks at the word. Scanning from left to right, it picks up the first letter of the word and stores it in the visual short-term memory. Then long-term memory is searched for phonemes associated with that particle. The computer says what it sees, and then the question is whether or not the process is complete. Has the whole word been pronounced yet? As long as the answer to that is "no," the operation continues.

If there were no constraints on short-term memory, and if there were a perfect one-to-one correspondence between graphemes and phonemes, this decoding task could proceed smoothly and easily. But instead, we must find ways of representing the devices learned by skilled readers to handle constraints and irregularities. One of them is a blending or chunking device. Readers put small units together into single larger units. Our program specifies that this integration is performed in auditory short-term memory, at least during an early stage of reading proficiency. We put a simple blending rule into the program: *If there are two things there, put them together.* But that is a very unsophisticated rule. What would the correct rules be? What are the natural, spontaneous blending heuristics of beginning readers? We do not know.

Once you have formed a new chunk, you must, of course, remember it. And then you must look back and see if what you have said is actually contained in the stimulus word. It turned out that this piece of code was the largest part of the program— suggesting that the programmer, who may be a surrogate child, had to do a lot of work to keep track of the flow in this part of the task. Having looked back and found confirmation, the computer says "I think I'm right." If disconfirmed, the computer would have said "I'm in trouble."

Figure 11 is a sample of a simulation run. First, the computer asks for input: "Type in the word you want me to pronounce." It is given the word *particular,* and then it produces a trace, or written record, of what it did. First, it registered the *p*, which is to say it noted that something already in its visual memory was in the word.

In response to the *p*, something in the computer's auditory memory was activated, the phonemic chunk *per*. It then fixated the *r*, and continued to scan. The letter *t* was registered, and the auditory memory fired *ta*. Then a blend occurred, because our simple rule was when you have two things in your auditory memory, put them together.

Then there was a storage or rehearsal operation, RE-MEMBER PERTA, but then the computer looked back to the beginning of the word again, and this time picked up a new particle, *part*, because there was no rule in the program that said if you already have the first part of a word, move on, do not start over. Because of that defect, a very scrambled situation develops, and the final output here is PARTPERPERTA. This was distressing to the simulators, until we realized that the output resembled the kind of stuttering that may occur in the beginning readers. Thus the computer serendipitously defined—not proved, but simply defined—one reason for this: failure to have a rule of the "don't start over" type.

The numbers shown on Figure 11 as Time:_____ will eventually reflect the times that we expect simulated operations to take. The numbers must incorporate, for example, eye movement times (300 msec per fixation); long-term memory search time; rehearsal time; articulation and pronunciation time; and so forth.

In general, this particular methodology forces us to come to terms with what we really believe to be true of the reading process. Unless we are willing to work at this level of detail, we are likely to use theoretical terms and concepts very carelessly, if comfortably. But if we take protocol data seriously and literally, if we think in terms of panoramic research data, and if we force ourselves to build models of what might be going on in the head of a reader, then we will be on the way toward APR Stage IV.

The Stage IIIA theorists and the Stage IIIB empiricists must join forces at just this point. What Stage IV will usher in is a complex, holistic, dynamic model of the reading process—each part of which is firmed up by hard numbers—such as the one reported by McConkie and Rayner (1975): 10 characters to the

```
START
TYPE IN WORD YOU WANT ME TO PRONOUNCE
PARTICULAR
     STATEMENT 17: VSTM = 'P',TIME =|183
     STATEMENT 22: ASTM = ' PER',TIME = 250
 PER
FIXATES THE R
     STATEMENT 17: VSTM = 'T',TIME = 450
     STATEMENT 22: ASTM = ' PER TA',TIME = 533
 PER TA
FIXATES THE A
     STATEMENT 27: ASTM = 'PER TA',TIME = 1350
     STATEMENT 27: ASTM = 'PERTA',TIME = 1417
PERTA
     STATEMENT 86: REMEMBER = 'PERTA-',TIME = 1467
     STATEMENT 31: REMEMBER = '',TIME = 1533
LOOKS BACK TO CHECK WORD
     STATEMENT 37: VSTM = 'PART',TIME = 1750
     STATEMENT 39: ASTM = '',TIME = 1833
     STATEMENT 22: ASTM = ' PART',TIME = 1950
 PART
     STATEMENT 43: REMEMBER = ' PART-',TIME = 2067
     STATEMENT 45: ASTM = '',TIME = 2133
     STATEMENT 17: VSTM = 'I',TIME = 2217
     STATEMENT 22: ASTM = ' I',TIME = 2333

 I
FIXATES THE I
     STATEMENT 17: VSTM = 'C',TIME = 2500
     STATEMENT 22: ASTM = ' I SER',TIME = 2583
 I SER
FIXATES THE R
     STATEMENT 27: ASTM = 'I SER',TIME = 2817
     STATEMENT 27: ASTM = 'ISER',TIME = 2850
ISER
     STATEMENT 88: VSTM = 'SI',TIME = 2950
     STATEMENT 89: ASTM = 'SI',TIME = 3100
     STATEMENT 90: REMEMBER = ' PART-SI-',TIME = 3167
     STATEMENT 91: ASTM = '',TIME = 3217
     STATEMENT 72: ASTM = ' PART',TIME = 3283
     STATEMENT 77: REMEMBER = '',TIME = 3383
     STATEMENT 17: VSTM = 'P',TIME = 3433
     STATEMENT 22: ASTM = ' PART PER',TIME = 3517
 PART PER
FIXATES THE R
     STATEMENT 27: ASTM = 'PART PER',TIME = 3767
     STATEMENT 27: ASTM = 'PARTPER',TIME = 3833
PARTPER
     STATEMENT 90: REMEMBER = 'PARTPER-',TIME = 3983
     STATEMENT 91: ASTM = '',TIME = 4033
     STATEMENT 72: ASTM = 'PARTPER',TIME = 4100
     STATEMENT 77: REMEMBER = '',TIME = 4200
     STATEMENT 17: VSTM = 'P',TIME = 4267
     STATEMENT 22: ASTM = 'PARTPER PER',TIME = 4317
PARTPER PER
FIXATES THE R
     STATEMENT 17: VSTM = 'T',TIME = 4950
     STATEMENT 22: ASTM = 'PARTPER PER TA',TIME = 5033
PARTPER PER TA
FIXATES THE A
     STATEMENT 27: ASTM = 'PARTPERPER TA',TIME = 5267
     STATEMENT 27: ASTM = 'PARTPERPERTA',TIME = 5333
```

Figure 11. Output of the simulation.

right of a fixation point can be picked up by skilled adult readers. If we can simulate reading, then we certainly have a theory of reading—a highly detailed theory. But a simulation cannot exist without the quantitative data that can only be obtained by careful experimentation. These numbers are the parameters of the reading process, they are the bones of a theory. Without a theory, empirical findings have a tendency to pile up in the corner, a heap that is soon forgotten. Theories pile up in a heap of their own across the room. One by one, then, psychologists may start the slow dance of APR Stage I all over again.

REFERENCES

Atkinson, R. C., Hansen, D. N., and Bernbach, H. A. 1964. Short-term memory with young children. Psychonomic Science 1:255–256.

Cohen, G. 1973. Hemispheric differences in serial vs. parallel processing. Journal of Experimental Psychology 97:349–356.

Davidoff, J. B., Cone, B. P., and Skully, J. P. 1978. Developmental changes in hemispheric processing for cognitive skills and the relationship to reading ability. In A. M. Lesgold, J. W. Pellegrino, S. Fokkema, and R. Glaser (eds.), Cognitive Psychology and Instruction. New York: Plenum.

Davis, F. B. (ed.) 1971. The Literature of Research in Reading with Emphasis on Models. New Brunswick, N. J.: Graduate School of Education, Rutgers State University. (Order from: Iris Corporation, P.O. Box 372, East Brunswick, N. J., 08816).

Dimond, S. J. 1971. Hemisphere function and word registration. Journal of Experimental Psychology 87:183–186.

Dimond, S., and Beaumont, J. 1971. Use of two cerebral hemispheres to increase brain capacity. Nature 232:270–271.

Dimond, S., and Beaumont, J. 1972a. Hemisphere function and color naming. Journal of Experimental Psychology 96:91–97.

Dimond, S., and Beaumont, J. 1972b. Processing in perceptual integration between and within the cerebral hemispheres. British Journal of Psychology 63:509–514.

Farnham-Diggory, S., and Gregg, L. W. 1975. Short term memory function in young readers. Journal of Experimental Child Psychology 19:279–298.

Farnham-Diggory, S., and Simon. H. A. 1975. Retention of visually presented information in children's spelling. Memory and Cognition 3:599–608.

Frederiksen, J. R. 1978. Assessment of perceptual, decoding, and lexical skills and their relation to reading proficiency. In A. M. Lesgold, J. W. Pelligrino, S. Fokkema, and R. Glaser (eds.), Cognitive Psychology and Instruction. New York: Plenum.

Geffen, G., Bradshaw, J. L., and Nettelton, N. C. 1972. Hemispheric asymmetry: verbal and spatial encoding of visual stimuli. Journal of Experimental Psychology 95:25–31.

Gregg, L. W. 1974. Perceptual structures and semantic relations. In L. W. Gregg (ed.), Knowledge and Cognition. Hillsdale, N.J.: Lawrence Erlbaum Associates.

Kolers, P. A. 1975. Pattern-analyzing disability in poor readers. Developmental Psychology 11:282–290.

Liberman, I. Y., Shankweiler, D., Liberman, A. M., Fowler, C., and Fischer, F. W. 1977. Phonetic segmentation and recoding in the beginning reader. In A. S. Reber and D. Scarborough (eds.), Toward a Psychology of Reading. Hillsdale, N. J.: Lawrence Erlbaum Associates.

Mackworth, J. F. 1971. Some models of the reading process: Learners and skilled readers. In F. B. Davis (ed.), The Literature of Research in Reading, With Emphasis on Models. New Brunswick, N. J.: Graduate School of Education, Rutgers State University.

Mayzner, M. S., Tresselt, M. E., and Cohen, A. 1966. Preliminary findings on some effects of very fast sequential input rates on perception. Psychonomic Science 6:513–514.

McConkie, G. W., and Rayner, K. 1975. The span of the effective stimulus during a fixation in reading. Perception and Psychophysics 17:578–586.

Miller, L. K., and Turner, S. 1973. Development of hemifield differences in word recognition. Journal of Educational Psychology 65:172–176.

Reddy, R., and Newell, A. 1974. Knowledge and its representation in a speech understanding system. In L. W. Gregg (ed.), Knowledge and Cognition. Hillsdale, N. J.: Lawrence Erlbaum Associates.

Roberts, G. R., and Lunzer, E. A. 1968. Reading and learning to read. In E. A. Lunzer and G. F. Morris (eds.), Development in Human Learning. New York: American Elsevier Publishing Company.

Rozin, P., and Gleitman, L. R. 1977. The structure and acquisition of reading. II. The reading process and the acquisition of the alphabetic principle. In A. S. Reber and D. Scarborough (eds.), Toward a Psychology of Reading. Hillsdale, N. J.: Lawrence Erlbaum Associates.

Rumelhart, D. E. 1977. Toward an interactive model of reading. In S. Dornic and P. M. A. Rabbitt (eds.), Attention and Performance VI. Hillsdale, N. J.: Lawrence Erlbaum Associates.

Samuels, S. J., and Anderson, R. H. 1973. Visual recognition memory, paired-associate learning, and reading achievement. Journal of Educational Psychology 65:160–167.

Seamon, J. G., and Gazzaniga, M. S. 1973. Coding strategies and cerebral laterality effects. Cognitive Psychology 5:249–256.

Spring, C., and Capps, C. 1974. Encoding speed, rehearsal, and probed recall of dyslexic boys. Journal of Educational Psychology 66:780–786.

Stanley, G., and Hall, R. 1973a. Short-term visual information processing in dyslexics. Child Development 44:841–844.

Stanley, G., and Hall, R. 1973b. A comparison of dyslexics and normals in recalling letter arrays after brief presentations. British Journal of Educational Psychology 43:301–304.

Swanson, H. L. 1977. Nonverbal visual short-term memory as a function of age and dimensionality in learning-disabled children. Child Development 48:51–55.

Torgesen, J., and Goldman, T. 1977. Verbal rehearsal and short-term memory in reading-disabled children. Child Development 48:56–60.

Vellutino, F. R. 1977. Alternative conceptualizations of dyslexia: evidence in support of a verbal-deficit hypothesis. Harvard Educational Review 47:334–354.

Vellutino, F. R., Steger, J. A., DeSetto, L., and Forman, P. 1975. Immediate and delayed recognition of visual stimuli in poor and normal readers. Journal of Experimental Child Psychology 19:223–232.

Venezky, R. L., and Calfee, R. C. 1970. The reading competency model. In H. Singer and R. B. Ruddell (eds.), Theoretical Models and Processes of Reading. Newark, De.: International Reading Association.

Witelson, S. 1976. Sex and the single hemisphere: specialization of the right hemisphere for spatial processing. Science 193:425–427.

Witelson, S. 1977. Developmental dyslexia: two right hemispheres and none left. Science 195:309–311.

CRITIQUE:
Information Processing:
A Model or Myth?
John T. Guthrie

James Stephens, the Irish writer, produced an unusual form of literature—fairy tales for adults. One of his bits of whimsy and wisdom opens with two philosophers living deep in a pine wood.

> Their faces looked as though they were made of parchment, there was ink under their nails, and every difficulty that was submitted to them, even by women, they were able instantly to resolve. The Gray Woman of Dun Gortin and the Thin Woman of Innes McGrath asked them the three questions which nobody had ever been able to answer, and they were able to answer them. That was how they obtained the enmity of these two women which is more valuable than the friendship of angels. The Gray Woman and the Thin Woman were so incensed at being answered that they married the two philosophers in order to be able to pinch them in bed, but the skins of the philosophers were so thick that they did not know that they were being pinched. They repaid the fury of the women with such tender affection that these vicious creatures almost expired of chagrin, and once, in a very ecstasy of exasperation, after having been kissed by their husbands, they uttered the fourteen hundred maledictions which comprised their wisdom, and these were learned by the philosophers who thus became even wiser than before (Stephens, 1912: 3–4).

One senses from Farnham-Diggory's presentation (this volume) that she believes information processing to be a latter-day philosopher capable of absorbing the many maledictions of reading.

Sylvia Farnham-Diggory opened her serious argument with Mackworth's model of skilled reading. This model has much to commend it. Out of the 48 information processing models reviewed by Geyer in the Reading Research Quarterly in 1972, this one has turned out to be the belle of the ball. Indeed, Geyer called it the "consensus of expert opinion in a number of fields concerning the identification and operational characteristics of information processing systems involved in reading" (1972:550).

With necessary oversimplification, Mackworth's model essentially contains three storage compartments: very short-term visual memory (iconic storage); short-term memory; and long-term memory. Conduits connecting these are called coding operations. Coding differs in nature (for example, acoustic vs. semantic) depending upon the location of the conduit. In the model, multiple feedback loops connect nearly everything to nearly everything else. Needless to say, no model of reading is totally comprehensive. But it seems worth reminding ourselves that reading would not be reading if it were not the processing of *language* in written form. In the Mackworth model, the language and meaning components seem overshadowed. The inclusion of the word "meaning" in the long-term memory box underestimates the complexity and importance of the psycholinguistic operations that occur during reading. One might claim that because language processing is not unique to reading, it should not be emphasized in a model of reading. However, language processing is not unique to spoken language either, and it certainly must be regarded as necessary, if not primary, to any guiding conceptualization of reading.

Farnham-Diggory raised a chilling question. Can the Mackworth model be tested? Certainly one quality of a good theory is that it is testable. It should be noted, however, that another quality of a good theory is that it is provocative. It should engender new models, hypotheses, and data. It is possible that the Mackworth model is more thought-provoking than testable.

Attempting to apply the Mackworth model to a specific illustration might be informative. For example, can the Mackworth model explain the behavior of one of the poor readers from Farnham-Diggory's chapter (see Table 1 therein) who was attempting to pronounce the word "particular"? One possible reason for some of the errors observed in this child is that visual sensory trace persisted too long, causing masking and confusion among the letters; another possible reason is that exit of information from iconic storage was delayed and the material was not coded in short-term memory efficiently; it may be that coding the visual stimuli to sound was inadequate; or it is possible that semantic memory of the child was limited, preventing the normal facilitation of word recognition that is partially based on semantic cues. Use of the model to analyze the protocol raises far more questions than it resolves. The model seems to be rather more evocative than explanatory. The power of making a scientific departure from a case study is that a host of theoretical and conceptual alternatives becomes immediately evident. With this type of a beginning, oversimplification is over.

There is a need to be wary of the representiveness of the protocol when engaging in a protocol analysis. Farnham-Diggory presented the case of a reading-disabled child. Her claim was that if a poor reader can be found to be deficient in a certain component of the reading process, then two birds have been killed with one stone. The theoretical benefit is that the component on which the reader was deficient has been confirmed as important in the model. The practical by-product is that remediation strategies may be implied by the finding. But suppose that the reading model does not account for the reading behavior of this one child's protocol. Is the model inadequate or is the protocol peculiar and anomalous? Does the limitation lie with the model or the data? If the model is questioned, a component of cognitive processing can be added to the model to account for this particular case. Because the component is interesting, a careful program of research on it can be initiated. Now the question raised is: are the new model and the new research general enough, that is, embracing a large enough proportion of the population, to be scientifically valuable?

It would certainly be unwise to modify a model based on one anomalous, bizarre case. But how often are individual cases bizarre? Two examples may be mentioned. Roger Brown (1970) has noted informally and without quantified observations, that the grammatical errors made by deaf children who are learning language are qualitatively different from errors made by normal two- and three-year olds. Surely the study of these errors would be useful for education of the deaf, but it may not shed light on normal development patterns. In studies of aphasia, Tallal and Percy (1973a; 1973b) found that children with receptive language disorders were markedly deficient in processing verbal and nonverbal auditory signals of short duration. For example, aphasics were deficient on the perception of stop consonants (information over 40 msecs) but were normal on perception of vowels (information over 250 msecs). This distinction regarding processing time does not seem enormously important for accounts of language development in normal children, although it is valuable for the study of aphasia. The suggestion here is that the variables that account for disorders of language or reading may be quite different from the variables that account for normal development.

It is the strong opinion of this writer that the scientific analysis of the deficiencies of poor readers is urgently needed; but it is primarily needed for the possible benefit it may bring to poor readers and secondarily needed for the by-products it may provide for theoretical accounts of reading in the normal population.

In conducting her protocol analysis, Farnham-Diggory makes the assumption that the child says what he saw. With this assumption, one could infer a great deal about visual processing from spoken output during reading. The viability of her assumption can be tested by looking at one error made by one child—the child read "instrument" when the word "estimate" was presented to him. It seems unlikely that he literally saw the word "instrument." He probably perceived a few cues—letters, letter fragments, perhaps word length—that elicited a meaningful word that was consistent with those visual and phonemic cues. The child probably expected a meaningful word, because other words in the list were meaningful. It seems plausible to me that what the child says is some combination of what he saw, what he expected to see, and what he knew before he looked (that is, what words were available in his memory to be elicited by a subsample of the total number of visual cues which are present in a given word). It is apparent that the Mackworth model does not provide ready explanations for all of the phonomena in these reading protocols. The protocols also do not serve to eliminate or verify beyond a reasonable doubt any components in the model. It seems that scientific progress depends on regularities within the protocols being identified, which means a large number of observations on one child or a smaller number over many children.

Farnham-Diggory suggests that one gift from information processing psychology to the field of reading is the strategy of converging data from many sources on one topical point of interest. Her example is the spelling styles of white and black children. She reported that because white children were faster in spelling words presented aloud than words presented in written form, they recode the printed stimulus into an auditory analogue and generate letters from the auditory form to spell the word. In contrast, black children perform faster when the word is given to them in printed form than when it is given in spoken form. Seemingly, black children used the visual memory as a basis for generating letters rather than recoding the visual material into auditory forms. How do these data converge on reading? Farnham-Diggory did not suggest an implication, but speculation seems possible. If the black children prefer long-term visual memory over long-term auditory memory for the storage of words, perhaps black children are relatively proficient in attaching meaning to visual cues in words. If a test of this hypothesis were positive, teaching strategies in reading that emphasized print to meaning associations might be tried with black children.

A methodology for the study of reading suggested by Farnham-Diggory was computer simulation. In the computer program she has worked on, the computer begins by looking at a word. It stores the first letter in visual short-term memory, searches long-term memory for the sound of the letter, searches for the next letter, retrieves the sound for that letter, combines the sound with the sound from the previous letter, determines whether or not a word has been completed; if not, the computer searches for the next letter. The process recycles until a word has been pronounced. As she acknowledges, this program has not been completely debugged, and its rendition of words is not yet perfected. But imagine that someone writes a program that is successful in instructing a computer how to pronounce words. Can it be assured that this program is the same one that informs the brains of children how to pronounce words? There are at least two criteria for an adequate simulation of reading: First, the components of the computer program should be the same as the components of human cognitive operations. For example, both would be expected to have visual short-term memories. Second, the parameters that influence one should influence the other. For instance, letter strings that are orthographically regular should be more quickly pronounced than letter strings that violate known orthographic rules. In the program developed by Farnham-Diggory and Gregg, serial processing of letters and word length will drastically affect the time required for word pronunciations; but word length is an extremely weak variable in affecting recognition accuracy or time for children (Lott and Smith, 1971). In addition, as Farnham-Diggory's protocols illustrate, children often say meaningful words when making errors, but with its present set of parameters, the computer program would not be likely to do that because a semantic storage system has not yet been incorporated.

It may be that a good simulation cannot be built without intimate knowledge of what is being simulated. NASA engineers can simulate the weightlessness of outer space because this condition consists of known principals of the physics of gravity. They know about the effects of weightlessness on the blood pressure of animals. With this knowledge they may simulate weightlessness and test its effects on human beings. But it would seem inefficient to begin creating one's concept of weightlessness by haphazardly trying different simulations of the condition. In reading there seems to be a need for many protocols and much experimental data, for example, about parallel processing of printed words, before simulations will be theoretically or heuristically optimal.

Buried in Farnham-Diggory's thinking is an assumption shared by many experimentalists that deserves to be disinterred, at least temporarily. The assumption is that if poor readers can be demonstrated to be deficient in one cognitive operation, an explanation of their disability or their low reading achievement has been discovered. If it could be shown that poor readers were depressed on one cognitive process but were normal on all others, this assumption would be tenable. But the data reveal that poor readers are worse than good readers of their same chronological age on a host of variables, including: 1) recall of discourse structure (Smiley et al., 1977); 2) sentence comprehension (Isakson and Miller, 1976); 3) word meaning retrieval (Golinkoff and Rosinski, 1976); 4) decoding speed (Perfetti and Hogaboam, 1975); 5) word recognition processes (Liberman et al., 1976); and 6) letter cluster detection (Kolers and Perkins, 1975). Being deficient in many operations, the poor readers' dilemma cannot be traced to any one variable. Apparently the predicament of poor readers is not due to a failure of one component, but is accompanied by failure in many components. Why many components should fail simultaneously is an important question. Whether poor reading can be traced to one deficient operation that in turn interferes with the others, or the simultaneous retardation of many operations, or other possible explanations will, it is hoped, be determined by future research.

The assumption of independent components in reading is especially pernicious for theory building. Independence is only one option. As Farnham-Diggory correctly remarks, the Rumelhart model of reading is a refreshing change. She emphasized the simultaneity of functions in his model, but the interactive characteristics should be emphasized as well. Components of reading, such as those in the previous paragraph, have influences from 6 to 1 (the traditional view) and from 1 to 6 (the contemporary one). For example, Anderson et al., (1977) show that discourse structure determines sentence recall; Anderson and Ortony (1975) show that sentence constraints influence the meanings that are recalled for the single words they contain. From here it is not too rash to suggest that higher-order operations could affect the decoding problems that Liberman et al. (1976) find among poor readers or the orthographic perception deficiencies reported by Katz (1977). To disentangle these relationships will require more than correlational studies that are the essence of current information processing paradigms. Learning studies of the early 1960s vintage may be needed to examine what happens to one component when another is increased in proficiency.

It would not be surprising if the performances of readers on cognitive components essential to the process were highly interactive. Such seems to be the case in language acquisition. Roger Brown, in *A First Language* (1973), anticipates some of his rich interpretations of developmental psycholinguistic data by saying that "order of development . . . is primarily determined by the relative semantic and grammatical complexity of the constructions" (p. 59). He shows that the acquisition of 14 morphological structures follows a nearly invariant sequence. But the morphemes increase in both semantic complexity (the number of semantic dimensions that they contain) *and* grammatical complexity (the number of transformations that can be made on them) at the same time. The performance of children on these two components of language, i.e., semantic complexity and grammatical complexity, is highly correlated. In reading, it is reasonable to suppose that decoding fluency, knowledge of word meanings, and discourse comprehension will develop interdependently.

The parting call from Farnham-Diggory was that the phenomenon of reading can be apprehended only when we can account for the protocols of individual children with dynamic, time-locked causal models of cognitive operations that are supported by experimental data and are verified by simulations, which is to say artificial devices that can read like humans. Beyond a doubt, these goals for the science of reading are themselves a philosophy of research for the future.

REFERENCES

Anderson, R. C., and Ortony, A. 1975. On putting apples into bottles—a problem of polysemy. Cognitive Psychology 7:167–180.

Anderson, R. C., Reynolds, R. E., Schallert, D. L., and Goetz, E. T. 1977. Frameworks for comprehending discourse. American Educational Research Journal 14(4):367–381.

Brown, R. 1970. Psychology and reading. In H. Levin and J. Williams (eds.), Basic Studies in Reading. New York: Basic Books, Inc.

Brown, R. 1973. A First Language. Cambridge, Mass.: Harvard University Press.

Geyer, J. 1972. Comprehensive and partial models related to the reading process. Reading Research Quarterly 7(4):541–588.

Golinkoff, R. M., and Rosinski, R. R. 1976. Decoding, semantic processing, and reading comprehension skill. Child Development 47:252–258.

Isakson, R. L., and Miller, J. W. 1976. Sensitivity to syntactic and semantic cues in good and poor comprehenders. Journal of Educational Psychology 68(6):787–792.

Katz, L. 1977. Reading ability and single-letter orthographic redundancy. Journal of Educational Psychology 69(6):653–659.

Kolers, P., and Perkins, D. 1975. Spatial and ordinal components of form perception and literacy. Cognitive Psychology 7:228–267.

Liberman, I. Y., Shankweiler, D., Liberman, A. M., Fowler, C., and Fischer, F. W. 1976. Phonetic segmentation and recording in the beginning reader. In A. S. Reber and D. Scarborough (eds.), Reading: Theory and Practice. Hillsdale, N. J.: Lawrence Erlbaum Associates.

Lott, D., and Smith, F. 1971. The independence of letter, word and meaning identification in reading. Reading Research Quarterly 6(3):394–415.

Perfetti, C. A., and Hogaboam, T. 1975. The relationship between single word decoding and reading comprehension skill. Journal of Educational Psychology 67:461–469.

Smiley, S. S., Oakley, D. D., Worthen, D., Campione, J. C., and Brown, A. L. 1977. Recall of thematically relevant material by adolescent good and poor readers as a function of written versus oral presentation. Journal of Educational Psychology 69(4): 381–387.

Stephens, J. 1912. The Crock of Gold. New York: Macmillan Company.

Tallal, P., and Percy, M. 1973a. Defects of non-verbal auditory perception in children with developmental aphasia. Nature 241:468–469.

Tallal, P., and Percy, M. 1973b. Developmental aphasia: impaired rate of non-verbal processing as a function of sensory modality. Neuropsychologica 11:389–398.

PERCEPTION IN THE ACQUISITION OF READING

Anne D. Pick

"Reading" and "reading disability" are frequent terms in the titles and discussion sections of papers published in journals in which studies of children's perception are reported. During the past decade many students of perceptual development have discovered in reading a concrete task in which general perceptual processes and activities are incorporated. To study the rich, complex task of reading in order to understand basic processes of perceptual development can only be advantageous in advancing our overall knowledge about perceptual development. It seems very likely that far more can be learned about human perceptual development by studying the perception of children learning to read than by studying the perception of children making judgments about line segments of various visual illusions. In other words, the position taken in this paper is that generalizable information about perceptual development will more likely be attained as a result of observing children in tasks that have more, rather than less, ecological validity.

The interest of students of perceptual development in reading can only be advantageous too in advancing our understanding of *reading*. Surely teachers and curriculum developers will be aided if they can communicate to researchers *what* it is that needs to be explained, and the researchers, in turn, can provide some of the general information that is potentially useful in making decisions about general principles of instruction or about individual children.

However, in order for this convergence of interests in understanding reading and in understanding perceptual development to be maximally productive, it may be that researchers have to conceive and conduct their experiments according to some specific principles of research strategy. The general consensus among both researchers and educational practitioners seems to be that many of the published papers on perception in reading provide rather little contribution to our understanding of reading. There also seems to be agreement, although this point seems less certain, that much of the published research on perception in reading also does little to further our understanding of perceptual development.

An earlier paper (Pick, 1970) attempted to assess the state of our knowledge about children's perception and learning to read. That paper included a discussion of some features that seemed to distinguish those studies that are informative about perception and reading from those that are less so. These characteristics seemed to depend on matters of research strategy. The arguments made in that paper will be reviewed here, so that the extent to which the state of our knowledge has changed during these five years can be assessed, and in order to make explicit the reasons for the type of research findings to be discussed subsequently in this paper.

A distinction can be made between reading as a complex *task,* and the *processes* that underlie performing that task. It is the processes that must be identified and understood, and obviously they can be inferred only from the task performance we can observe. In order to study those basic processes that underlie reading, researchers construct experimental tasks that are considerably simpler than the reading task itself. This is done so that the effects of the relevant process can be examined in a setting simpler than the complex reading task. However, because the goal is to understand the basic processes in reading, it must be assumed that the experimental task is a small piece or "slice" of reading. In other words, because it is desirable to interpret the observations from the experimental task as being informative about reading, it must be assumed that the processes whose effects are observed, in fact, are those that function in reading. A sizable number of published studies share features that make this assumption difficult to maintain.

One such feature is illustrated in studies of intermodal matching, that is, recognizing the equivalence of the same information whether presented visually or aurally. In such studies the experimental tasks often take the form of assessing children's skill in recognizing the equivalence of dot patterns presented via various modalities (e.g., Birch and Belmont, 1965; Blank and Bridger, 1966; Beery, 1967; Ford, 1967; Sterritt, Martin, and Rudnick, 1969). These studies were conceived on the basis of the very reasonable hypothesis that intermodal matching might be important in reading acquisition because learning to read requires that children learn a visual presented system of information that corresponds to the aural system they already understand and use. Accordingly, children's skill in recognizing the equivalence of patterns of dots presented via different modalities and in various spatial and temporal patterns was assessed in relation to their reading achievement. Some presentation conditions seemed more difficult than others, but in general, the relationships between performance on these tasks and reading were low and inconsistent, suggesting that the relevant perceptual processes were not, in fact, basic to reading. But perhaps it is unreasonable to suppose that if reading requires intermodal matching, then *any* task that requires intermodal matching will reflect the same intermodal processes that occur in reading. Reading does not, after all, require matching dot patterns. Because the experimental task, dot pattern matching, does not closely resemble reading, the intermodal processes in the two tasks may well differ. A good research strategy, if one wants to understand perceptual processes in reading, may be to construct experimental tasks that resemble as closely as possible some aspect of reading. A feature shared by too many studies of perception and reading is an experimental task quite unlike any aspect of reading. Another example of this problem is found in studies of the role of perceptual decentration in reading in which the experimental tasks are designed without regard to the fact that written language is not composed of arbitrary strings of letters, but instead has structure (Elkind, Horn, and Schneider, 1965; Elkind, Larson, and van Doorninck, 1965; Elkind and Deblinger, 1969).

How can studies be conceived and designed so as to maximize the possibility of yielding useful information about perceptual processes in reading? One strategy frequently used is to let the subjects define the appropriate tasks. Good and poor readers perform a variety of tasks and those tasks on which their performance differs are identified as the tasks requiring perceptual processes relevant for reading—processes that are inadequate in the poor readers. The logic of this strategy is straightforward and intuitively reasonable. One need only assume that the difference in perceptual functioning of the two groups is a function of the characteristic defining the groups, that is, skill in reading. However, this assumption is difficult to maintain, for, as Meehl (1967) and others have pointed out, human attributes do not come singly and independently. By the time a child has been identified as a poor reader that child is likely to differ in a variety of ways from children who are good or even adequate readers, and not all of these differences are accounted for by such statistical variables as mental age, IQ, and socio-economic status. Many differences are ones that we would predict would affect children's performance on a test-like task—for example, motivation, test-taking skills, school-related anxiety. It should be expected that good and poor readers would differ in performance on a great many tests, and indeed, the list of supposed basic perceptual processes in reading that have been identified using the strategy of comparing good and poor readers is long. It includes intermodal integration, perceptual decentration, shifting attention between modalities (Busby and Hurd, 1968), orientation discrimination (Wechsler and Hagin, 1964), recognition of embedded figures (Stuart, 1967), finger localization or finger differentiation (Reed, 1967; Satz and Sparrow, 1970), visual-verbal integration (Vellutino et al., 1975), visual or auditory encoding (Senf, 1969), impulsivity as a cognitive style (Kagen, 1965), and visual-motor integration (Frostig, 1964).

The strategy of comparing good and poor readers in order to identify basic processes in reading has been extended in a way that seems rather dangerous, although there is not a great deal of evidence to support this judgment. The extension is to argue that because comparisons of good and poor readers have allowed identification of important perceptual processes in reading, screening instruments can be constructed so as to identify, perhaps as early as preschool, those children who later may have reading problems. Those children can then be given remedial assistance to prevent them from becoming reading failures.

The fault in this argument is the assumption that perceptual "problems" associated with reading difficulties in children at a given age are also problems when observed in younger children. An example of this is found in the case of letter and word reversals. Some children who are poor readers confuse the orientation of letters and of parts of words. They write words with letters in incorrect orientations; they write words from right to left; they write or read words with letters in incorrect positions, as in the confusion of *was* with *saw*. However, there is no basis for assuming that inattention to orientation differences among preschoolers is predictive of later reading problems. Many preschool children do not discriminate letter orientation when they first learn to produce and identify letters and to write their names (e.g., Gibson, Gibson, Pick and Osser, 1962). An hypothesis suggested a number of years ago for why children do not discriminate orientation differences still seems reasonable now (Gibson, Gibson, Pick, and Osser, 1962). Children's experiences with objects do not lead them to use orientation differences as a basis for distinguishing among objects. In fact, orientation must be ignored in recognizing the identity of an object. Such is obviously not the case with letters; however, the child learning about letter shapes has no more reason to use orientation as a basis for identification of letters than for objects until the child learns that letters are different. The child learning about letters has to learn that an additional feature (orientation) that was ignored for object identification has to be taken into account in establishing letter identification. For a letter to be produced "correctly," it must not only be composed of the appropriate pattern of lines or curves, but it must also be in a particular orientation. Before diagnostic devices are used to identify potential reading problems among preschoolers, at least it should be established that failure to attend to orientation differences (or some other "failure") is predictive of subsequent difficulty in learning to read. The lack of predictive information seems not to have hampered the development of such diagnostic devices, however (e.g., Lefford, Birch, and Green, 1974).

If comparing good and poor readers is not the best strategy for identifying important perceptual processes in reading, what is a productive strategy? A strategy that seems reasonable is one that is based on a theory or conceptual analysis of what one is studying. Such a strategy is productive, from a conceptual analysis of reading, because it is possible to construct experimental tasks that are "slices" of reading. Also, when experimental questions asked are based in theory, then the findings from any particular study are informative not just about performance on the particular experimental task used, but about the whole set of questions with which the theory is concerned. Theories help to identify the particular questions to be asked about reading, and the answers to the questions help to refine the theories themselves as well as provide new information about the nature of reading.

During the past five years of research on reading, it seems that there has been a marked increase in the recognized relevance of theory for understanding the role of perception and other processes in reading. Currently, there are several important models of reading—either about all of reading or about one aspect of reading, such as word perception. Important models are those that are generating research that is leading to a better understanding of the process of reading.

Most current models are about skilled reading, rather than about the acquisition of reading. One example of such a model is Hochberg's hypothesis testing model of reading (Hochberg, 1970) in which the skilled reader successively: 1) peripherally locates an important or informative portion of text; 2) fixates that portion; 3) confirms (or disconfirms) a hypothesis about the information contained in that portion; and 4) generates a hypothesis about where, in the periphery, the next important portion of the text is located. Another example of a model of skilled reading is Gough's model of "one second of reading" (Gough, 1972). According to this model, to identify a printed word the reader: 1) fixates his or her eyes; 2) produces a visual image, or icon, of the word; 3) identifies the letters; 4) transforms the letters into a phonemic representation; and 5) identifies the word from a word store or lexicon. The word is then stored briefly in memory to be integrated with the other words of the sentence. Other current important models of the same part of reading, word recognition by skilled readers, are those of Rubenstein, Lewis, and Rubenstein (1971a; 1971b) and of Spoehr and Smith (1973; 1975).

LaBerge and Samuels (1974) have constructed a model of reading that they are applying to reading acquisition. Briefly, their model, like those just summarized, involves a series of steps by which written text is processed until its meaning is identified. First, letter patterns are identified via feature detectors. Then the letters are organized into units like words. Finally, the meaning of the word is accessed when the word is phonologically recoded; the phonological "code" is associated directly with the meaning. An important aspect of skilled reading, according to LaBerge and Samuels (1974), is that the skills associated with each of these stages are automatic, in that they do not require attention after the appropriate codes have been learned. LaBerge and Samuels are actively engaged in work with young children in school who are learning to read, and an important focus of their work with children is to train automaticity of various subskills thought part of skilled reading.

The authors of other models of skilled reading also see implications of their models for teaching reading. For instance, Rubenstein et al. noted:

> It seems to us that our findings have some relevance for at least one controversy in the teaching of reading—specifically with regard to the question whether the whole-word or phonic approach is more effective . . . . The finding that phonemic recoding is involved in word recognition supports the phonic approach . . . . (1971b:655).

Although the specific features of these summarized models vary, they share at least one implicit assumption about reading acquisition, which is that beginning reading is an unskilled or immature form of skilled reading. The task of the child who is learning to read is to practice and perfect those skills that constitute skilled reading; the acquisition of reading *is* the acquisition of the skills that characterize the adult reader. As Hochberg expressed this view: "there are a number of very different response systems that change as a result of acquiring skill at directed reading, but there's no reason to believe that there's any change in what the reader actually sees at any glance" (Hochberg, 1970:78).

A different view of the acquisition of reading occurs when the theory being applied to reading acquisition is a theory about development. For one thing, from a theory about development different hypotheses are generated about what the phases or stages of learning to read might be. The difference may be apparent in an analogy of learning to read a second language as compared to learning to read a first language. For instance, a skilled reader of one language must actively work at inhibiting the imposition of the structure of that language onto the language being learned. The relevant *prior* knowledge differs for the two tasks of learning to read a second or a first language, including prior knowledge of the nature of the criterion task itself. A second appropriate analogy may be a comparison of reading acquisition by hearing and by deaf children. A theory about reading acquisition by hearing children may not predict very well how deaf children learn to read because the relevant prior knowledge or basic skills differ for hearing and deaf children. In fact, deaf children may very likely learn to read differently from the way hearing children learn to read; at least, this is an hypothesis suggested by the facts that it is difficult for deaf children to learn to read, and that their eventual level of reading competence tends to be low (Furth, 1966).

To put the point simply, a theory explicitly about development does not necessarily describe a beginning reader as a deficient or naive skilled reader. For that reason, which is obviously a matter of judgment based on one's intellectual upbringing, this author's research on reading acquisition, and the research most relevant to it, tends to be generated by theories about development rather than by theories or models of skilled reading. The most detailed example of a productive relationship between a theory of development and our understanding of the role of perception in reading acquisition is found in Eleanor Gibson's theory of perceptual learning and development and the decade and a half of research on reading that the theory has generated.

According to Gibson, there are at least three clearly identifiable trends in the perceptual development of children (Gibson, 1969). These trends include: 1) increasingly precise correspondence between stimulus differences and a child's perceptual discrimination of those differences; 2) increasingly efficient and systematic attention; and 3) increasingly economical perceptual functioning. All three trends have implications for investigating and for understanding beginning reading (Gibson, 1974; Gibson and Levin, 1975).

An obvious skill that a beginning reader must acquire early is letter discrimination. In order to learn to read, a child must be able to discriminate among the letter shapes. This skill is related to the first trend in perceptual development, and several studies conducted early in Gibson's program of research on reading were concerned with the course of development of discrimination among letter shapes—when it occurs and what is its basis. The findings of these studies are well known; it was demonstrated that confusions among unfamiliar letter-shapes decrease with age (Gibson, Gibson, Pick, and Osser, 1962), and that improvement in discrimination of them is based on detecting and using their distinctive features (Pick, 1965). The length of time required for young children to decide that two letters are different is directly related to the number of distinctive features distinguishing between them (Gibson, Schapiro, and Yonas, 1968).

The purpose of many prereading exercises is to direct children's attention to the types of distinctive features that distinguish among letters. Although it is unclear that the perceptual discriminations required to successfully perform these exercises in fact do transfer to reading (Rosen and Ohnmacht, 1968; Silberberg, Iverson, and Silberberg, 1968), the exercises themselves are based on the assumption that discriminating and identifying letter shapes is an important early step in learning to read.

However, although letter discrimination is an important early aspect of formal reading acquisition, it is certainly not the only important foundation for learning to read. Many people have pointed out that an important fact about most young children who are learning to read is that they are already skilled users of a spoken language (e.g., Gibson, 1969; Pick, 1970). Models of reading describe the relationship between what is learned during reading acquisition, and the spoken language that the child already knows. This relationship may take the form of specific reference to a lexicon of words to describe how printed words are recognized and identified (e.g., Gough, 1972) or to some other procedure of acquiring meaning from written words (e.g., LaBerge and Samuels, 1974). Alternatively, the relationship may take the form of an assumed analogy between understanding speech and understanding printed text (e.g., Hochberg, 1976) or of a general reference to reading as consisting of decoding written text into the spoken language that it represents (e.g., Fries, 1962).

In any case, all the models of reading that have been proposed to date acknowledge explicitly that the language that children have acquired prior to formally learning to read is an important basis for what it is that they learn when they learn to read. The fact that deaf children *can* learn to read does not render unreasonable the assumption that knowing and using a language ordinarily is important in determining how learning to read occurs. The processes in reading acquisition for a deaf child may be quite different and the fact that deaf children typically are retarded in reading suggests that this may be so.

Knowledge of spoken language may not just be important in determining what is learned when one learns to read. In other words, the importance of the spoken language may not lie only in the relationship that exists between written and spoken language. There may also be aspects of a child's knowledge *about* language that are important for his or her early reading acquisition. This is similar to what Mattingly (1972) and others (e.g., Savin, 1972) have termed "linguistic awareness," although as

Mattingly uses the term, he seems to mean one's awareness of one's own linguistic activity. Such awareness is only one aspect of a person's general knowledge about language.

Several students at the University of Minnesota (Celia Brownell, John Drozdal, Marita Hopmann, Jeff Lockman, and Marsha Unze) and this author have recently been trying to identify some specifiable aspects of a child's knowledge about language that may be relevant for being able to learn to read. It seems that perception plays a large part in defining this relevant knowledge about language because a fundamental characteristic of this linguistic awareness has to do with treating language as an object. Long before a child learns to read he or she has to have differentiated language noises from other noises. It is reasonable to hypothesize that the child does this by discovering and detecting those features distinguishing language noises and their sources from other noises and their sources. There is a good deal of evidence now that very young infants treat human speech sounds as special sounds (Eimas et al., 1971; Moffitt, 1971; Morse, 1972; Horowitz, 1975). For instance, babies of less than three months of age can attend to sounds that represent changes in voice tone quality, and can distinguish between their mothers' voice and a stranger's voice (Horowitz, 1975).

Another thing that children might have to know about language before they can learn to read is that language *can* be represented on paper in two dimensions. Most children in many cultures have much exposure during their first few years of life to paper, to books, to pages, and to pictures as representations. Before a child can learn to read, it may be necessary to distinguish between the form in which language is represented in two dimensions and the form in which other things are represented. In other words, the child may have to begin to detect the distinctive features of printed text as compared to pictures or to lines and curves on paper that are not printed text. Young preschool-age children who sit with story books "reading" them aloud—saying strings of words that may or may not have to do with the story text in the book—may be learning about the particular type of two-dimensional shapes that represent spoken language. Likewise, the preschool children who scribble on paper and then come to a teacher or parent with the question, "What does this say?"—and who are frustrated by an explanation that it does not say anything—seem to be engaged rather actively in seeking out the features that distinguish writing from lines and curves that are not writing.

Two students, Celia Brownell and Marita Hopmann, and this author are making observations about what characteristics define printed words for young children who are either prereaders or who are in an early phase of formal reading instruction. Children are shown strings of letters and asked simply to judge whether or not the strings are words. The letter strings vary in several ways. Some are, in fact, words. Some contain letters that are incorrectly oriented—either right-to-left reversed, or upside down, or rotated 90°. Some strings are orthographically illegal; for example, they consist of four consonants and no vowel or four vowels and no consonants. Some strings contain too many letters to be one word. An attempt is being made to determine those features that identify printed words for children who do not yet read, and how new features are used to more precisely define printed words as children learn to read. Testing is being done using preschool-age children and kindergartners who vary from having little knowledge of reading to having some reading skill; a few older children who do know how to read are also being tested.

As yet, judgments from only a few children have been obtained; however, those few children have provided consistent information. The youngest children, nursery school children who for the most part do not know how to read any words, judge all of the strings to be words except those that are too long, that is, those that contain too many letters to be a word. Nursery school children who know how to read a few words judge both strings that are too long and strings that contain letters rotated 90° or upside down as not being words. Children of first grade and older for the most part judge only the real words as being words, though they point out that some strings, for example, *amde,* or *baot* are words if the letters are rearranged.

Thus, even children who do not yet know how to read base judgments of word-likeness on features, such as length, that distinguish between words and non-words. As children acquire rudimentary reading skills, they use more of the available features to distinguish between words and non-words, and their identification of what is a word becomes more specific and precise. Of course, such observations do not allow the claim that knowledge of word properties is an essential prerequisite for learning to read, but the observations are in accord with such an hypothesis. If these observations continue to be reliable with more children, they provide another clear example of the type of increasingly precise differentiation of things, in this case word-like things from non-word-like things, that characterizes perceptual development.

Another type of knowledge about language that may be relevant for reading acquisition is the knowledge that speech can be segmented into units of varying temporal duration—phrases, words, perhaps syllables and phonemes. Apparently young children find it relatively easy to segment spoken words into syllables (Savin, 1972) and considerably more difficult to segment words into phonemes (Calfee, Chapman, and Venezky, 1970; Gibson and Levin, 1975). It may be worthwhile to ask, do children have to be able to break up speech into segments smaller than words in order to learn to read easily, or is the acquisition of skill in segmenting speech into units smaller than words an outcome of beginning to learn to read? In any case, knowledge that there are segments of speech, that there are segments of print that correspond to segments of speech, and that these segments can be smaller even than single words, seems important knowledge for early reading acquisition.

These more or less isolable speech sounds, syllables, and phonemes, are represented in printed words by single letters or small combinations of letters. Because these are units that can be recombined according to a set of rules to form new words, they might be units that are abstracted during the course of learning to read. We know that adults, as well as children who have had some reading instruction, perceive legal strings of letters, e.g., *BLASPS*, more easily than they perceive illegal strings of the same letters, e.g., *SPSABL* (Gibson, Pick, Osser, and Hammond, 1962; Gibson, Osser, and Pick, 1963). Skilled readers have abstracted units of words that correspond to invariant spelling-sound relations. They have, in short, learned about the structure of printed words—an instance of the third general trend in perceptual development described by Gibson, the trend toward increasingly economical perceptual functioning.

Whether syllables or phonemes or some other unit of spoken words are more relevant for learning to read is not known. One way to find out is to observe the units of printed words that children learn when they first learn to read words. Several students (Celia Brownell, John Drozdal, Marita Hopmann, Marsha Unze) and this author have completed a study in which an attempt was made to find out what if any units of printed words are detected and used by children who are first beginning to learn to read.

Kindergartners were taught to read twelve words, the first words they ever read, and then they were asked to read some additional words in order to see what they had learned about the training words in the course of learning to read them. The twelve training words that were taught the children were the following: BUM, HUM, BUG, HUG, RAT, FAT, RAN, FAN, SIP, LIP, SID, LID.

The seventeen children who participated in the study were selected from two kindergarten classrooms on the basis that they demonstrated knowledge of some single letter-sound relationships, and that they were unable to read any words. These children represented about one-third of the children in the two classes. Another third of the children already knew how to read some words, and the other third knew little about letters and sounds represented by letters. We were trying to select children who were on the verge of learning to read, but who did not already know how to read any words.

The teaching occurred during four training sessions conducted individually with each child over a period of four days. During the first session, the child learned four words; for example, BUM, HUM, BUG, HUG. During the second session, the child reviewed those words and learned four new words; for example, RAT, FAT, RAN, FAN. During the third session, the child reviewed all the words previously learned and learned the final four words; for example, SIP, LIP, SID, LID. During the fourth session, the child reviewed all the words and when he or she correctly read all twelve words, he or she was shown some new words, and the transfer phase of the procedure was begun.

Each of the four students collaborating in the study taught and tested some of the children. Although teaching methods obviously affect what children learn, no attempt was made to control the method so carefully that any transfer effect might be a result of the method used to teach the children. Consequently, very general procedures were developed that would be used by all four teachers, but decisions about how to teach a given child were left to each teacher's judgment. The sessions were all tape-recorded in order to later examine any teacher/tester effects and also in order to assess what strategies seemed especially appropriate or inappropriate.

Caricature outline drawings, one to represent each training word, were used as motivating devices in teaching the words initially. The pictures were not used as mediating devices, but only as devices to attract and keep the children's interest in the learning task. Consequently, drawings were used in initially presenting words to the children, but they all performed the criterion task, that is, read through the list of twelve words accurately, without the drawings. The transfer words did not have drawings to accompany them, and these words were presented as some new words that the children could try to read because they had done so well with the words they had already learned.

There were eighteen transfer words, composed of the same medial vowels and the same initial and final consonants of which the training words were composed. Many of the words were nonsense words—the children were simply told that some of the new words were "funny" words, and that it would be fun to try to read them anyway. Many of the children seemed aware that the words didn't "mean" anything, but this did not appear to disturb the children as they tried to read the "words."

There were three types of transfer words, and six words of each type. One type, labeled Type I, were composed of initial consonant-vowel combinations that were the same as the combinations of the training words, and a different final consonant.

A second type of words, labeled Type II, were composed of final vowel-consonant combinations that were the same as the combinations of the training words, and a different initial consonant.

The third type of transfer words, labeled Type III, were also composed of the same consonants and vowels as the training words, but the combinations differed from the combinations of which the training words were composed. The transfer words used in the study, according to type, were:

Type I	Type II	Type III
HUN	FUM	BAP
BUP	SUG	HIN
FAM	LAT	RIM
RAD	HAN	FUD
LIT	BIP	SUT
SIG	RID	LAG

Because all of the transfer words were composed of the same initial consonants, medial vowels, and final consonants as the training words, the children had had equivalent experience with the separate single letter-sound relationships of the transfer words. The transfer words varied in terms of whether they shared a consonant-vowel (Type I) or vowel-consonant (Type II) combination with the training words. It seemed reasonable that if, during learning to read the training words, the children began to abstract units larger than single letter-sound relationships, then it should be easier for them to read the Type I or the Type II words than to read the Type III words. Depending upon whether the unit abstracted with the initial consonant-vowel, or the final vowel-consonant, either Type I or Type II words should be easier to read than Type III. Obviously, if both initial consonant-vowel and final vowel-consonant units were abstracted, then both Type I and Type II words might be easier to read than Type III words. And, if the children had not abstracted any useful unit larger than a single letter-sound relationship, Type III words should be just as easy for the children to read as Type I and Type II words.

For the transfer phase, children were shown the eighteen transfer words in an unsystematic order, and were asked to read them. The children were praised for a correct reading. They were also praised and encouraged for an incorrect reading by such statements as "That's really close; that's a good try. Let's try it again and see if you can get even closer." After an incorrect first reading, the children were encouraged to make one or two more attempts at a word. The primary criterion for deciding when to go on to the next word was the teacher's judgment about the child's motivation. The goals were for the children to try to read all the words, to read them as best they could, but not to feel frustrated.

The teachers wrote down what the children said for each word, and the sessions were also tape-recorded just as the training sessions had been. Subsequently the senior investigator listened to all of the tapes and transcribed the responses. These written observations were compared with those of the teachers and any disagreements were resolved by having another of the teachers listen to the tapes. There were few disagreements— only eight in all for the written transcriptions of the children's first tries.

Questions of interest included how the children read a word initially, and also how they made successive attempts to read the word if the initial attempt was incorrect. As it turned out, most of the analyzable information was obtained from the children's initial attempts to read a word. The experimenters varied greatly in the amount and type of active encouragement they provided for children to work on a word. For instance, some children eventually said a word correctly because the experimenter had said it first. Other children, seemingly equally proficient, never said a given word correctly because the experimenter avoided saying the actual word during the attempts to support and encourage the child.

Thirteen children correctly read some of the words on the first attempt during the transfer phase. The children read more Type I words correctly than Type III words (sign test, $p = 0.004$, two-tailed). They did not read significantly more Type II words correctly than Type III words (sign test, $p = 0.124$, two-tailed). In addition, the total number of Type I words read correctly on the first try was 27; the total number of Type II words read correctly on the first try was 14; and the total number of Type III words read correctly on the first try was 9.

These results suggest that the children did begin to abstract useful units larger than single letter-sound relationships. The first units that they began to abstract were at the beginnings rather than at the ends of words. The initial consonant-vowel combinations of the words they had learned in training were used in reading the new transfer words, but the final vowel-consonant combinations of the training words were not. To put it in Sesame Street parlance: the children learned about the HU__, BU__, RA__, FA__, SI__, and LI__ "families"; they did not learn about the __UM, __UG, __AT, __IP, __AN, and __ID "families."

The children's errors in reading the transfer words, that is, the words incorrectly read on the first try, are also informative about what aspects of the training words are being used to try to read the transfer words. The error patterns, like the pattern for words read correctly, suggest that initial combinations of words previously learned are useful in reading new words. A relevant comparison is the distribution of words in which the initial combination is read correctly (and only the final consonant is wrong) with the distribution of words in which the final combination is read correctly (and only the initial consonant is wrong). That distribution is shown as Table 1.

Table 1. Number of transfer words incorrectly read on first try in which initial combination or final combination was correct

Type	Initial consonant-vowel correct	Vowel-Final consonant correct
Type I	15	1
Type II	4	5
Type III	7	4

The type of error in which the initial consonant-vowel combination is correct occurs largely in Type I words and, of course, those are the words in which the same initial consonant-vowel combinations are maintained from the training words. The type of error in which the final vowel-consonant combination is correct only occurs a few times in Type II words, however, despite the fact that those words share the final vowel-consonant combinations with the training words. Again, these error patterns provide evidence that the children used the initial combinations of the training words in trying to read the transfer words. They did not similarly use the final combinations in trying to read the transfer words.

In general the first part of the word was much more likely to be correct than was the last part of the word. Few of the children's reading errors for words of any type were errors in which the last part of the word (either the vowel and consonant or the final consonant) was read correctly, but the first part was not. In contrast, many of the children's reading errors (77 in all) were errors in which the first part of the word (either the consonant and vowel or the consonant) was read correctly, but the last part was not.

One important question is whether the initial consonant-vowel relationships of the training words transferred intact because the children could not segment them into phoneme-like sounds, or because they had been abstracted as a unit. Two pieces of evidence may be used to argue for the latter answer.

First, if the transfer from reading training words to reading new words as simply the passive transfer of letter combinations that cannot be segmented, and are not really useful, then we might not expect to see the pattern of correct reading corresponding to the pattern of errors as well. In other words, the fact that more Type I words were read correctly than Type II or Type III suggests that the children had learned something that they were indeed using. It was easier to get even the difficult final portion of a new word correct if the initial combination was familiar (that is, if it was Type I) than if that initial combination was new.

The second piece of evidence about whether the units were abstracted or simply unsegmentable comes from children who had a special type of difficulty reading the transfer words. A few children in our study were very good at "sounding out" the new words but still they could not read them correctly. One such child sounded out correctly every single transfer word, and did not read even one of the words correctly, either on a first or subsequent try. He would often sound out the word quite fast, but he still could not read it. Other children also sounded out the new words *and* read many of them correctly. Both types of children can segment perfectly well, but one reads the words correctly, and the other cannot. I think the contrast between the children suggests that those who can read the words have abstracted a unit that is available to be used in reading the new words.

Some preliminary observations have been made about what units of words are salient for judging word similarity for individuals of varying levels of reading skill. These observations are striking in their concordance with the findings about the importance for early readers of patterns in the first part of the word. Children and adults, ranging in age from 4 to 44, were asked to compare two pairs of printed words and to judge which pair has members that are more similar to each other. The pairs of words used so far are words from the training words of the reading study. One type of pair consists of words that differ only in the final consonant: FAT–FAN, BUM–BUG, HUM–HUG, SIP–SID, RAT–RAH, LIP–LID. The other type of pair consists of words that differ only in the initial consonant: SIP–LIP, BUG–HUG, SID–LID, RAT–FAT, BUM–HUM, RAN–FAN. In this experiment subjects are shown two pairs of words, one pair from each list, and asked to say which pair has members more alike; for example, FAT–FAN or SIP–LIP. Each person judges six sets of words and the results to date are striking in their consistency. Skilled readers, from 8 to 44 years of age, quickly and consistently (that is, for all six sets of pairs) say that pairs like RAT–FAT or BUM–HUM are more alike than pairs

like RAT−RAN or BUM−BUG. Further, they are consistent in
the reason for their choice: the pairs that are judged more alike
are the pairs that rhyme. One child in this group first said the
pairs were the same because they each varied by one letter, and
then she said, "Oh yes, these (indicating the "rhyming" pairs)
are more alike because they change one letter *and* they rhyme."
The *sound* of the words is the feature on which similarity is
based for these readers.

The younger, less skilled readers judge similarity differently, however. They quickly and consistently judge pairs like
RAT−RAN or BUM−BUG as more alike than pairs like
RAT−FAT, or BUM−HUM. They explain that the reason for
their judgment is that the "first part" of the word is the same.
Some of these children have gone through the procedure a second time with the experimenter reading aloud the words instead
of just showing the child the printed words. When they hear the
words instead of reading them, these children judge FAT−RAT
pairs to be more alike than BUM−BUG pairs, and their judgments, like those of the skilled readers reading the words, are
based on the fact that words that are alike at the end—that they
rhyme.

The patterns upon which early readers base judgments of
word similarity when they read are patterns at the front of the
word—and those are also the patterns that seem to be abstracted
and transferred from the first words children learn to read. For
skilled readers, the patterns upon which judgments of word similarity are based are at the end of the word, and they have to do
specifically with sound relations. If these observations are reliable with more subjects and more words, they provide further
evidence about the importance of the first part of words in determining how beginning readers read printed words.

Finally, an attempt will be made in this paper to explore the
question of how meaning is acquired from printed words, and if
it is acquired differently by beginning and by skilled readers.
Although this question is not exclusively about the role of perception in reading acquisition, it is relevant because it has to do
with the information that is acquired from printed words and
whether or not that information is the same for readers of varying
levels of skill. The answer to the question of whether or not
meaning is acquired from printed words similarly by skilled and
by early readers is not yet clear, but some recent evidence

suggests an answer that is different than the answer generally accepted only a short time ago. There previously seemed to be rather compelling evidence that meaning is acquired from printed words differently by beginning readers and by skilled readers; specifically, that beginning readers acquire meaning from printed words by mapping the words into their spoken representations, whereas skilled readers acquire meaning directly from the printed version (Gibson, Barron, and Garber, 1972; Gibson, 1974). Such an interpretation implies that beginning readers acquire information about meaning by decoding printed words. However, there is evidence recently obtained that meaning in printed words may be acquired by early readers, at least as early as second grade, in a way similar to that used by skilled readers (Barron and Urquhart, 1975). Furthermore, Golinkoff and Rosinski (1976) have made the intriguing suggestion that decoding and acquiring meaning may be separate skills for word recognition. They found that third- and fifth-grade children who were not skilled decoders still acquired meaning from printed words, presumably in the same way as their peers who were skilled decoders. Golinkoff and Rosinski suggested that decoding may not be a necessary intermediate step toward acquiring the meaning of a printed word. This might be true, at least for words that children can decode, and it raises the interesting possibility that after children learn the *idea* of decoding when they are learning to read, further emphasis on decoding per se instead of on learning the relevant graphic units for maximum efficiency in acquiring meaning may be uneconomical.

CONCLUSIONS

Knowledge about perceptual development is increased by investigating the role of perception in the task of learning to read. Much is already known about children's perception in controlled laboratory settings. Relatively much less is known about children's perception in a multi-leveled task like reading, which is more complex than tasks typically used in the laboratory, but which is representative of tasks undertaken by children in their daily functioning.

Furthermore, knowledge about perceptual development as it is organized into a theory furthers an understanding of what it means to learn to read. The theory provides a framework of hypotheses and experimental operations to guide the choice of questions to ask about reading. Such an organized context in which to study reading is important because collections of unrelated empirical facts cannot, by themselves, provide a coherent explanation of such a complex task as reading. A related advantage of studying reading in the context of a theory is the possibility of extending our understanding to other types of reading as well. For instance, limited information exists about how children read music, read maps, and read pictures. A theory can provide a common basis for systematic investigation and interpretation of similarities and differences among such tasks. At least such an approach is plausible, given the acknowledged mutual interests of teachers and researchers in understanding how children learn to read and what it is they learn.

REFERENCES

Barron, R. W., and Urquhart, S. M. 1975. Two hypotheses about access to the meanings of words and pictures. Paper presented at the biennial meeting of the Society for Research in Child Development, April, Denver.

Beery, J. 1967. Matching of auditory and visual stimuli by average and retarded readers. Child Development 38:827–833.

Birch, H., and Belmont, L. 1965. Auditory-visual integration, intelligence and reading ability in school children. Perceptual and Motor Skills 20:295–305.

Blank, M., and Bridger, W. 1966. Deficiencies in verbal labeling in retarded readers. American Journal of Orthopsychiatry 36:840–847.

Busby, W., and Hurd, D. 1968. Relationships of auditory and visual reaction times to reading achievement. Perceptual and Motor Skills 27:447–450.

Calfee, R. C., Chapman, R. S., and Venezky, R. L. 1970. How a Child Needs to Think to Learn to Read. Technical Report No. 131. Madison: Wisconsin Research and Development Center for Cognitive Learning.

Eimas, P. D., Siqueland, E. R., Jusczyk, P., and Vigorito, J. 1971. Speech perception in infants. Science 171:303–306.

Elkind, D., and Deblinger, J. 1969. Perceptual training and reading achievement in disadvantaged children. Child Development 40:11–19.

Elkind, D., Horn, J., and Schneider, G. 1965. Modified word recognition, reading achievement and perceptual decentration. Journal of Genetic Psychology 107:235–251.

Elkind, D., Larson, M., and van Doorninck, W. 1965. Perceptual decentration learning and performance in slow and average readers. Journal of Educational Psychology 56:50–56.

Ford, M. 1967. Auditory-visual and tactual-visual integration in relation to reading ability. Perceptual and Motor Skills 24:831–841.

Fries, C. C. 1962. Linguistics and Reading. New York: Holt, Rinehart and Winston.

Frostig, M. 1964. The Marianne Frostig developmental test of visual perception, 1963 standardization. Perceptual and Motor Skills 19:464–499.

Furth, H. G. 1966. A comparison of reading test norms of deaf and hearing children. American Annals of the Deaf 3(2):461–462.

Gibson, E. J. 1969. Principles of Perceptual Learning and Development. New York: Appleton-Century-Crofts.

Gibson, E. J. 1974. Trends in perceptual development: implications for the reading process. In A. Pick (ed.), Minnesota Symposia on Child Psychology, Vol. 8. Minneapolis, Minnesota: University of Minnesota Press.

Gibson, E. J., Barron, R. W., and Garber, E. E. 1972. The developmental convergence of meaning for words and pictures. In appendix to final report, The Relationship Between Perceptual Development and the Acquisition of Reading Skill. Project No. 90046, Grant No. OEG-2-9-420446-1071 (010), between Cornell University and the United States Office of Education.

Gibson, E. J., Gibson, J., Pick, A., and Osser, H. 1962. A developmental study of the discrimination of letter-like forms. Journal of Comparative and Physiological Psychology 55:897–906.

Gibson, E. J., and Levin, H. 1975. The Psychology of Reading. Cambridge, Mass.: M.I.T. Press.

Gibson, E. J., Osser, H., and Pick, A. 1963. A study of the development of grapheme-phoneme correspondences. Journal of Verbal Learning and Verbal Behavior 2:142–146.

Gibson, E. J., Pick, A., Osser, H., and Hammond, M. 1962. The role of grapheme-phoneme correspondence in the perception of words. American Journal of Psychology 75:554–570.

Gibson, E. J., Schapiro, F., and Yonas, A. 1968. Confusion matrices for graphic patterns obtained with a latency measure. The Analysis of Reading Skill: A Program of Basic and Applied Research. Final Report, Project No. 5-1213, Contract No. OE6-10-156, between Cornell University and the United States Office of Education.

Golinkoff, R. M., and Rosinski, R. R. 1975. The access of printed word meaning by children and adults. Paper presented at the biennial meeting of the Society for Research in Child Development, April, Děnver.

Gough, P. B. 1972. One second of reading. In J. F. Kavanagh and I. G. Mattingly (eds.), Language by Ear and by Eye. Cambridge, Mass.: M.I.T. Press.

Hochberg, J. 1970. Components of literacy: speculations and exploratory research. In H. Levin and J. P. Williams (eds.), Basic Studies on Reading. New York: Basic Books, Inc.

Hochberg, J. 1976. Toward a speech-plan/eye movement model of reading. In R. Monty and J. Senders (eds.), Eye Movement and Psychological Processes. New York: Halstead Press.

Howowitz, F. D. 1974. Visual attention, auditory stimulation, and language discrimination in young infants. Monographs of the Society for Research in Child Development, 39 (5 and 6, Serial No. 158).

Kagan, J. 1965. Reflection-impulsivity and reading ability in primary grade children. Child Development 36:609–628.

LaBerge, D., and Samuels, S. J. 1974. Toward a theory of automatic information processing in reading. Cognitive Psychology 6:293–323.

Lefford, A., Birch, H. G., and Green, G. 1974. The perceptual and cognitive bases for finger localization and selective finger movement in preschool children. Child Development 45:335–343.

Mattingly, I. G. 1972. Reading, the linguistic process, and linguistic awareness. In J. F. Kavanagh and I. G. Mattingly (eds.), Language by Ear and by Eye. Cambridge, Mass.: M.I.T. Press.

Meehl, P. 1967. Theory-testing in psychology and physics: a methodological paradox. Philosophy of Science 34:103–115.

Moffitt, A. R. 1971. Consonant cue perception by twenty- to twenty-four-week-old infants. Child Development 42:717–731.

Morse, P. A. 1972. The discrimination of speech and nonspeech stimuli in early infancy. Journal of Experimental Child Psychology 14:477–492.

Pick, A. D. 1965. Improvement of visual and tactual form discrimination. Journal of Experimental Psychology, 69:331–339.

Pick, A. D. 1970. Some basic perceptual processes in reading. Young Children 25:162–181.

Reed, J. 1967. Lateralized finger agnosia and reading achievement at ages 6 and 10. Child Development 38:213–220.

Rosen, C., and Ohnmacht, F. 1968. Perception, readiness, and reading achievement in first grade. Perception and Reading, pp. 33–39. Proceedings of the Twelfth Annual Convention of the International Reading Association, Newark, Del.

Rubenstein, H., Lewis, S. S., and Rubenstein, M. A. 1971a. Homographic entries in the internal lexicon: effects of systematicity and relative frequency of meanings. Journal of Verbal Learning and Verbal Behavior 10:57–62.

Rubenstein, H., Lewis, S. S., and Rubenstein, M. A. 1971b. Evidence for phonemic recoding in visual word recognition. Journal of Verbal Learning and Verbal Behavior 10:645–657.

Satz, P., and Sparrow, S. 1970. Specific developmental dyslexia: a theoretical reformulation. In D. J. Bakker and P. Satz (eds.), Specific Reading Disability: Advances in Theory and Method. Rotterdam: University of Rotterdam Press.

Savin, H. B. 1972. What the child knows about speech when he starts to learn to read. In J. F. Kavanagh and I. G. Mattingly (eds.), Language by Ear and by Eye. Cambridge, Mass.: M.I.T. Press.

Senf, G. M. 1969. Development of immediate memory for bisensory stimuli in normal children and children with learning disorders. Developmental Psychology, Monograph 1, (6, Pt. 2).

Silberberg, N., Iversen, I., and Silberberg, M. 1968. The predictive efficiency of the Gates Reading Readiness Tests. Elementary School Journal 68:213−218.

Spoehr, K. T., and Smith, E. E. 1973. The role of syllables in perceptual processing. Cognitive Psychology 5:71−89.

Spoehr, K. T., and Smith, E. E. 1975. The role of orthographic and phonotactic rules in perceiving letter patterns. Journal of Experimental Psychology:Human Perception and Performance 104:21−34.

Sterritt, G., Martin, V., and Rudnick, M. 1969. Sequential pattern perception and reading. Reading Disability and Perception, pp. 61−71. Proceedings of the Thirteenth Annual Convention of the International Reading Association, Newark, De.

Stuart, I. 1967. Perceptual style and reading ability: implications for an instructional approach. Perceptual and Motor Skills 24:135−138.

Vellutino, F. R., Smith, H., Steger, J. A., and Kaman, M. 1975. Reading disability: age differences and the perceptual-deficit hypothesis. Child Development 46:487−493.

Wechsler, D., and Hagin, R. 1964. The problem of axial rotation in reading disability. Perceptual and Motor Skills 19:319−326.

CRITIQUE:
Translating Research in Perception and Reading into Practice

John J. Pikulski

In the first pages of her paper, Pick reopens a controversy that remains quite unsettled in scholarly circles—the relationship that should exist between practitioners and researchers. "Perception in the Acquisition of Reading," the preceding chapter in this book, is definitely written from the perspective of a researcher who is concerned with better understanding the phenomenon of human perceptual development. In contrast, the perspective of this writer is that of a practitioner, someone who has almost daily contact with teachers who are continuously forced to deal with reading in its full complexity, rather than being afforded the opportunity—perhaps even the luxury—of being able to focus selectively upon some "small slice" of the reading process. It seems unfortunate that professionals in fields of study that deal with human behavior often divide clearly into practitioners on one hand and scientists (experimenters, theorists) on the other. Crossing from one camp to the other occurs only with great difficulty. The scientist, in pursuing his or her goal of extending empirical evidence, and in the name of controlled experiment, must often deal with topics that are esoteric or oversimplified in nature; on the other hand, the practitioner is faced with the need to make day-to-day large-scale decisions that can seriously affect the lives of human beings— decisions that can't wait for an empirical base or the results of a well-designed experiment. Not only is it difficult to be both practitioner and scientist, it often seems that there is little potential for one group of professionals to be of help to the other. The empirical findings or theories of the scientist are often rejected as irrelevant or lacking in definitiveness by the practitioner; the clinical activities of the practitioner are often viewed with disdain by the scientist. The problem is not a new one. Almost ten years ago, Shakow (1969) wrote: "The scientist... has tended to view the clinical psychologist, with the psychiatrist and social worker, as grubbers in the soil of service" (p. 6). Surely the teacher, the teacher educator and the educational practitioner in general would qualify for inclusion in the "grubber" category.

Although not engaging in the evaluative dimension referred to in the statement by Shakow, Kerlinger recently restates a view that scientific research can be, and perhaps should be, independent of its practical implications. "If we are to understand the influence that research can have in educational practice, we must understand how misguided the pragmatic view is. No amount of Congressional, government or university student actions and demands can change the stubborn fact that scientific research of any consequence never pays off directly" (Kerlinger, 1978:13). In that same publication, Popham appears to be expressing an almost opposite position when he writes: "The time has definitely arrived for us to reconceptualize the method of inquiry into education so that it contributes more directly to the improvement of education practice. . . what is surprising is the persistence of many educational researchers to persevere in traditional, low-yield forms of inquiry" (Popham, 1978:2).

Pick's position seems intermediate between the two outlined above. She calls for teachers and curriculum developers to communicate to researchers what it is that needs to be explored and researchers in turn will provide information that may become useful in making decisions about principles of general instruction or about individual children. This appears to be a rather weak position that recommends a rather limited interaction. Stronger statements like that by Popham seem needed, as are suggestions like those made by Krathwal (1978), who calls for very lively interaction between researchers and practitioners in which the latter attempt to validate or invalidate, in a naturalistic setting, results obtained by the former under the necessary but artificial controls of a laboratory. Although studying children's perceptions of isolated three-letter sequences, some of which are words and some of which are non-words, may have greater ecological validity for the study of perception than studies that ask children to make judgments about line segments of visual illusions, the task remains quite low in "ecological validity" for studying the process of learning to read. There is the definite need for researchers of perception as it applies to reading to interact more actively with practitioners who can help to determine the validity and stability of experimental findings.

Nevertheless, Pick's introductory comments are most help-ful; although her conclusion that "many of the published papers on perception in reading provide rather little contribution to our understanding of reading" (Pick, this volume) seems an under-statement from the perspective of an "applied" researcher or practitioner, her call for research strategies that involve experi-mental tasks that as closely as possible resemble some aspect of reading, if heeded, might help. In addition, however, to looking carefully at the character of the stimuli to be used in such studies, experimenters should also give serious thought to using a greater range of stimuli within a study in order to justify making generalizations. For example, will generalizations built from studies focused upon nonsense syllables composed of three capi-tal letters (as in Pick's work) hold for three-letter meaningful words and slightly longer words? Likewise, many of the ex-perimenters observe children's behavior over a very short period of time. Efforts should be made to determine if observed experi-mental efforts are stable and durable.

Finally, though it is obviously necessary for purposes of ex-perimental control to work with only small pieces or "slices" of reading, efforts should be made to then observe what happens when increased complexity is introduced. For example, much of the study of perceptual processes and reading focuses on single word units. Would results be meaningful if the child were to read contextual materials, or is context so powerful a variable that it vitiates the effects found in experiments with single words? If it is, those observed phenomenon may have little practical implica-tion. Thus the experimental tasks described by Pick remain rather artificial and low in ecological validity. Her position re-garding the called-for interaction between practitioners and ex-perimenters appears to need extension. It is to be hoped that the suggestions of Krathwal will be heeded and attempts will be made to extend findings obtained in laboratory-like settings to more naturalistic settings involving reading tasks more like those that children encounter when learning to read.

Pick's discussion of the difficulty in identifying important perceptual processes in reading is useful and is based on valid information. She appropriately rejects the comparisons of popu-lations of good and poor readers as an illegitimate procedure for isolating essential processes. Dykstra's (1966) review of an allied topic, the role of auditory discrimination and its effect on read-ing, also suggested that this approach could lead to distorted interpretations. Dykstra's conclusions were drawn from studies that were more applied than theoretical in nature. Using the results of studies based on such comparisons is particularly inappropriate when planning and implementing preventive programs for young children or remediation programs for disabled readers.

Pick also rejects as inappropriate investigations that use non-reading tasks in an attempt to investigate processes thought to underlie reading, and she uses the study of children's skill in recognizing the equivalence of dot patterns through both visual and auditory modalities as an illustration of such an approach. On the basis of her review of the literature she concludes that "the relations between performance on these tasks and reading were low and inconsistent, suggesting that the relevant perceptual processes were not, in fact, basic to reading" (Pick, this volume). It is interesting to note, however, that two very recently published research reports that included a review of the literature (Rae, 1977; Ward, 1977) both conclude that there is a significant relationship between performance on intermodal matching tasks and reading achievement. However, it seems also possible to conclude that even their own data fail to support their conclusions. For example, in the Rae study, the correlation between intermodal matching and reading achievement was only 0.19 when the effects of intelligence were controlled. Although the relationship was statistically significant ($p < 0.05$), there would appear to be no practical significance to a task that explains less than four percent of the variance in reading achievement. Pick's conclusions then stand firm in this area.

In reference to the topic of identifying the essential perceptual processes, there is some evidence to suggest that whether or not a child has a visual perception problem is based upon how visual perception is measured, and certainly visual perception is measured in a variety of ways (Barrett, 1965; Smith, 1968; Krueger, 1975). For example, Pick makes reference to perceptual orientations that appear in a child's writing. Writing, however, involves a less direct measure of perception than does a matching task, because the former calls for an integration of perception, memory, and fine motor control. Reading certainly seems immediately dependent on perception and memory, but not so much on fine motor control. The Bender Gestalt Test (Bender, 1938), which is almost certainly the most frequently used means for officially labeling a child as being perceptually deficient, requires discrimination skills plus fine motor productions. Yet a study by Zach and Kaufman (1972), using the Bender Gestalt figures, found little relationship between kindergarten children's performance on a multiple-choice matching task that required primarily perceptual skills and performance on a standard administration that required both perceptual and fine motor skills. The correlation between the two was only −0.19.

Therefore, a need exists for researchers to help in making a clear differentiation between those tasks that require perception, as in matching and discrimination tasks, those that require perception plus memory, and those that involve both of the former plus fine motor skills. Unfortunately, these distinctions are frequently not made. In some of her earlier writings, Pick (1965) discusses differences that occurred in tasks requiring successive comparisons, tasks requiring discrimination and memory, and simultaneous comparisons that required similar discriminations but not memory. Different factors seemed to influence performance on the same tasks. More work involving such comparisons and more consistent use of clear terminology is badly needed.

It is difficult to challenge Pick's contention that experimentation aimed at identifying essential perceptual processes should ideally be tied to a theoretical framework, because the potential payoff is much greater. However, an expansion of her definition of what important models are seems in order. She defines important models as those that are generating a great deal of research that seems to be contributing to a better understanding of reading. Certainly, sheer volume of research is not a sufficient criterion for evaluating a theory. From a practitioner's point of view, one criterion that does seem reasonable as a reflection of "contributing to a better understanding of reading" is that the results can be translated into meaningful implications for improving the efficiency with which children can learn to read. That's not to say that research that does not have immediate instructional implications is not of value; in some cases, its value may not be recognized, as was the case with the discovery of the transitor. Nevertheless research that has demonstrable implications deserves credit.

There is the need also to be cautious about becoming overly enamored with theoretical models or positions. They can get out of hand, as Farnham-Diggory suggested in another chapter of this book. Solley and Murphy took rather a strong stand in their book, *The Development of the Perceptual World* (1960), where they wrote, "We are *not* going to present a full-fledged theory; our tentative guesses are our only theory. Premature theories cloud both issues and data, and serve little, except to allow authors to believe in the magical power of their words" (p. 15). Theoretical development in reading frequently does not seem to yield promising results; Pick implies this in her criticisms of theories that view beginning readers as immature skilled readers and of theories of general development. Unfortunately, Pick fails to convince her readers that Gibson's Theory of Perceptual Learning, which she cites as particularly promising, has led to a better understanding of reading. Although it may have been beyond the scope of "Perception in the Acquisition of Reading" to present a full and convincing presentation of that theory, Ruddell (1977), in a review of a full exposition of that theory, concludes that the phrase "too vaguely specified to be checked" applies to Gibson's theory as well as other theories of reading.

Therefore, although the hope remains that a comprehensive theory of reading acquisition will develop, it does not appear to exist at this time. Calling for such a theoretical structure is appropriate, but research that is problem centered, that seeks pragmatic solutions to pressing problems, should neither be discouraged nor denigrated simply because it is not couched in a theoretical framework.

Pick is very cautious in the extent to which she draws practical implications for reading instructions from research results. She therefore avoids some pitfalls that are common. She did cite an illustration of other researchers (Rubenstein, Lewis, and Rubenstein) drawing a practical implication from a research-related theory of reading. Rubenstein, Lewis, and Rubenstein drew themselves into what they called ". . . one controversy in the teaching of reading—specifically with regard to the question of whether the whole-word or phonic approach is more effective. . . " (1971; from Pick, this volume). Unless there is substantial context that alters and qualifies this statement, it would have to be labeled as simply out of touch with reality. The either/or question of whole word vs. phonics is as outdated as the question of whether heredity *or* environment influences human behavior. Certainly, practitioners are beyond the either/or question, and no widely accepted current approach to teaching reading advocates using either a whole-word *or* phonics approach; rather, popular approaches to teaching reading differ on the relative emphasis placed on each. Likewise, the conclusion that "The finding that phonemic recording is involved in word recognition supports the phonic approach" (Rubenstein, Lewis, and Rubenstein, 1971; from Pick, this volume) is extraordinarily oversimplified; there is no one phonic approach, but instead numerous approaches to phonic instruction.

Pick offers good argument for her conclusion that there is potentially serious difficulty in theories or models that view the beginning reader as a deficient adult reader, and that much is to be gained by looking at children developmentally; however, too often researchers working from a developmental point of view seem to pay inadequate attention to the types of experience and training that young children have had. For example, when studying young children's perception of a word, Dr. Pick and her students found that at even the earliest levels, they rejected strings of letters that were too long to be words. Very interestingly, Meltzer and Herse (1969) found that prereaders rejected *actual* long words as words and Downing (1974) recently found that in studying the child's concept of a spoken word, children rejected long spoken words as being words. He concluded that for his study, the error of rejection was due to the facts that the children were being introduced to reading, that only short words were used in their reading materials, and that the teacher had labeled only these as words. His conclusion was that the children had developed a faulty *concept* of words as a result of their educational experiences. Thus, what may appear a natural developmental-perceptual phenomenon, may, in fact, be a reflection of experience of training.

Pick and her colleagues did seem aware of this dimension in that they did work with preschool youngsters who could not read, as well as those in the beginning stages of reading acquisition; nevertheless, even the preschoolers may have brought with them a variety of experiences with reading materials as a result of their interaction with parents and siblings. The confounding of results is even more possible in the study that Pick described in detail wherein children were taught three letter "words" and then asked to identify transfer "words." Again the experimenters seem to deny possible influences due to past teaching and they indicate that the children were learning their first words as part of the experiment. However, the significant amount of past experience kindergarten children have had with reading is witnessed by Pick's report that one third of the class could already read and another third had developed "some knowledge of sound-symbol relationships."

In conclusion, it seems that the gap between researcher and practitioner, between research and practice, is still very wide with reference to the topic of perception as it applies to reading. It is to be hoped that, through more frequent interaction between researchers and practitioners, this gap can be narrowed.

REFERENCES

Barrett, T. 1965. The relationship between measures of prereading visual discrimination and first grade reading achievement: a review of the literature. Reading Research Quarterly 1(1):51–76.

Bender, L. 1938. A Visual Motor Gestalt Test and Its Clinical Uses. New York: American Orthopsychiatric Association.

Downing, J. 1974. The child's conception of "a word." Reading Research Quarterly 9(4):568–582.

Dykstra, R. 1966. Auditory discrimination abilities and beginning reading achievement. Reading Research Quarterly 1(3):5–34.

Kerlinger, F. 1978. Back to Basic? Misconceptions of educational research. Partnership 3(1):12–13.

Krathwal, D. 1978. Improving educational research and development. Partnership 3(1):6–7.

Krueger, L. 1975. Familiarity effects in visual information processing. Psychological Bulletin 82(6):949–974.

Meltzer, N. S., and Herse, R. 1969. The boundaries of written words as seen by first graders. Journal of Reading Behavior 1:3–14.

Pick, A. D. 1965. Improvement of visual and tactual form discrimination. Journal of Experimental Psychology 69:331–339.

Popham, J. W. 1978. The leader's column. Partnership, 3(1):2.

Rae, G. 1977. Relation of auditory-visual integration to reading and intelligence. Journal of General Psychology 97:3–8.

Rubenstein, H., Lewis, S. S., and Rubenstein, M. A. 1971. Evidence for phonemic recoding in visual word recognition. Journal of Verbal Learning and Verbal Behavior 10:645–657.

Ruddell, R. 1977. Review: The Psychology of Reading. Harvard Educational Review 47(3):442–444.

Shakow, D. 1969. Clinical Psychology—As Science and Profession. Chicago: Aldine Publishing Co.

Smith, H. K. (ed.) 1968. Perception and Reading. Newark, De.: International Reading Association.

Solley, C., and Murphy, G. 1960. Development of the Perceptual World. New York: Basic Books.

Ward, L. 1977. Variables influencing auditory-visual integration in normal and retarded readers. Journal of Reading Behavior 9(3):290–295.

Zach, L., and Kaufman, J. 1972. How adequate is the concept of perceptual deficit for education. Journal of Learning Disabilities 5:351–356.

THE ACQUISITION OF LITERACY BY CHILDREN AND ADULTS

Thomas G. Sticht[*]

It seems appropriate in this book, whose title is The Acquisition of Reading, to attempt to better understand the relationship of reading to the broader concept of *literacy*. Much of the concern for reading is expressed as concern for literacy—the problem being that many people in our society, and in developing third-world societies, are illiterate or unsuitably literate for the demands of modern civilization. As Miller has put it:

> On the one hand, knowledge is becoming increasingly necessary for survival, and literacy is the key tool for the acquisition of that knowledge. On the other hand, the teaching of reading in our public schools—especially in the ghettos, both urban and rural—is failing badly, and all subsequent education built on reading fails with it. (1972:376)

In addition to expressing the ever-increasing need for literacy in a world burgeoning with knowledge, and in which the gathering, synthesizing, and generation of new knowledge provides some of the more lucrative opportunities for employment, Miller expresses the generally held view of literacy as "the key tool" for acquiring knowledge. He then implies that because the teaching of reading is so bad, many people do not learn to read well, and because reading is a major part of literacy, and because literacy is required for acquiring the knowledge offered by the educational system, many people will not be able to acquire that knowledge and will be ". . . barely tolerated at a level of existence we call 'welfare' " (Miller, 1972:375).

* The author is with the Basic Skills Group of the National Institute of Education. The ideas and opinions expressed herein are his own and do not represent the opinions and/or policies of the National Institute of Education or the Department of Health, Education, and Welfare. The research described here was completed while the author was with the Human Resources Research Organization, Monterey, California. Thanks to HumRRO colleagues Larry Beck, John Caylor, and Bob Hauke for helpful comments in the preparation of this paper.

131

PROBLEMS IN
UNDERSTANDING THE NATURE OF LITERACY

The way in which we conceptualize the nature of reading and its relationship to literacy will determine the types of training and education programs we develop, and the types of research programs we pursue to contribute to the solution of reading and literacy problems. For this reason we need to have as clear an understanding as possible of what we mean by literacy and reading, and how these concepts relate to the acquisition of knowledge.

Evidence abounds that indicates that there is currently considerable lack of consensus as to what literacy means, and how knowledge, reading, and literacy interrelate. For example, here is an item from the National Assessment of Educational Progress: Reading (1972).

The person being tested is presented the following sign:

HORSEPOWER without HORSE SENSE	IS FATAL

They are then asked: Where would you probably see this sign? (They are given the instruction to mark the correct alternative.)

		Percent Correct by Age			
		9	13	17	Adult
On a highway	X	23.3	44.6	75.7	88.4
On a gymnasium floor	—				
At a racetrack for horses	—	64.3	47.2	17.6	7.0
		(Percent choosing this alternative)			
In a grocery store	—				
I don't know	—				

The point to remember about this item is that it occurred within an assessment battery that purports to assess our nation's achievement in *reading;* those who marked the third alternative would be scored incorrect and their reading capability, and hence the nation's reading capability, would be challenged. Yet in this study, and others like it of recent vintage (Murphy, 1975; Northcutt, 1975), there is no check to find out whether lack of reading skill or lack of specific knowledge is the prime reason for lack of correct performance on many items. Presumably, if the problem was solely one of not being able to comprehend the *written* message, then the respondent would have no trouble in selecting the correct answer if the message were presented in *spoken* form.

In a recently completed project for the United States Office of Education, Adult Education Division (Northcutt, 1975:44), literacy was conceived of as "composed of an application of the communications (reading, writing, speaking, listening), computation, problem solving, and interpersonal relations skills to the general areas of occupational knowledge, consumer economics, community resources, government and law, and health"! In this case then, literacy is not *a* "tool skill" for acquiring knowledge, as Miller states; rather, it is a *set* of "tool skills" *plus* knowledge of particular content domains. This project has produced a set of test items similar to many of those in the National Assessment of Educational Progress (NAEP), in that they fail to distinguish between lack of reading ability and lack of knowledge. Yet, important conclusions about *reading* are reached based upon such ambiguous data—"About one-fifth of the sample could not *read* an equal opportunity notice well enough to identify a verbal statement which defined its meaning" (Northcutt, 1975; italics mine). In this study, one-fifth of this adult sample would suggest that 20+ million adults have a serious *reading* problem! Today the results of this study are being widely used to design curricula for adult literacy programs.

A major difference between the perspectives of educational researchers, such as those cited above, and a large number of other researchers in regard to the nature of reading, and hence the nation's "reading problem," is succinctly presented by Jenkins and Liberman (1972):

> At all events the 'reading problem' as we know it would not exist if, in dealing with language, all children could do as well by eye as they do by ear (p. 1).

According to this view, in which writing is construed as an alternative input display to speech, the "reading problem" is one of getting children to learn the knowledge of sight-sound correspondences, and to develop skill in using this knowledge to the point of being able to comprehend printed messages with the same degree of accuracy and efficiency as they could comprehend the message if it were presented in spoken form.

From the foregoing, it seems that many researchers have wished to limit the concept of literacy to that of an alternative, graphic, method of representing the spoken language (writing) and to learning to comprehend the graphic representation of language (reading) by eye as well as one could previously comprehend the acoustic representation of language by ear. (The text edited by Kavanagh and Mattingly, 1972, contains a fairly representative sample of researchers who have been participants in the large-scale Project Literacy effort and other efforts where the focus has been on reading as "decoding print to speech.")

Although educators and lay persons have also included the notions of "reading as a substitute for listening to spoken language" within their concept of literacy, they have further expanded the meaning of "reading" to include the knowledge of "general" vocabulary and concepts and the learning of new skills for perceiving information from graphic displays (tables, graphs, maps, etc.), which involve both linguistic and non-linguistic features. Thus, as in the NAEP example above, and in various "reading" tests, students can score low in "reading" because of their lack of specific vocabulary or other knowledge, their lack of skill in processing information from special graphic displays, or their lack of skill in languaging by eye as well as they can by ear (as well as other factors, such as low motivation, etc.). Furthermore, "reading" training programs usually go well beyond simply teaching the encoding and decoding into graphic material of what one already knows, and include the teaching of specific knowledge in various content areas. Thus, the term "reading training" is regarded as synonymous to "literacy training."

A GENERAL MODEL OF
THE DEVELOPMENT OF LITERACY SKILLS

Because of the confusion regarding "reading" and "literacy," with its frequent detrimental effects in the assessment, teaching, and researching of reading, I have found it useful to conduct research and development projects on the design of literacy training programs following the conceptual guidance of a simple model of the major components and processes involved in the development of literacy skills.

In this section, the model of the development of literacy skills as given in Sticht et al. (1974) is described and some evidence for the model's general validity is presented. Next, some research based on the model that we have used with children and adults is discussed. The first study describes research to assess discrepancies between auding and reading skills of adults in a literacy training program. The second study concerns the measurement of automaticity in decoding in children and adults who are in literacy training. These studies suggest that learning to language by eye as well as one can language by ear may take considerably longer than we thought.

The Developmental Model

Figure 1 presents the developmental model of literacy in schematic form. Briefly, the model formally recognizes what common sense tells us, and that is that when a child is first born, he or she is born with certain Basic Adaptive Processes (BAP) for adapting to the world around them. These BAP include certain

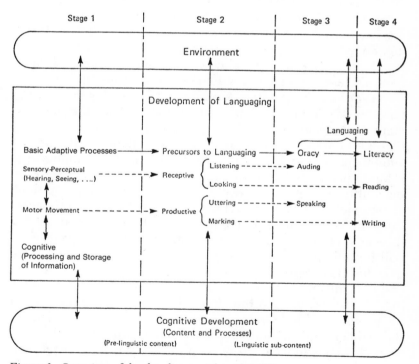

Figure 1. Overview of the developmental model of literacy.

information processing capacities for acquiring, storing, retrieving, and manipulating information. This stored information processing capacity forms a cognitive content that in its earlier forms is pre-linguistic (Figure 1; Stage 1). After some time, though, the child develops skills for receiving information representing the cognitive content of others, and for representing his own cognitive content to others. This is accomplished through the specialization of the information processing activities of listening, looking, uttering, and marking (Figure 1; Stage 2). The specialization is for the use of these skills for the express purposes of externally representing one's own thoughts for others to interpret, and forming internal representations of the external representations of others' thoughts. More specifically, though, the particular specialization of present concern is the representation of thoughts via the use of conventionalized signs (words) and the rules for sequencing these signs (syntax) in speaking and in auding (listening to speech in order to language) (Figure 1, Stage 3).

Finally, if the child is in a literate society, he may acquire the specialized looking and marking skills of reading and writing. For present purposes, we presume that we are talking about the "typical" case in our literate society, and assert that children typically learn to read and write (Figure 1, Stage 4).

A further aspect of the developmental model is that it holds that the development of the oracy skills requires the development of the cognitive content through the intellectual activity that we call conceptualizing ability. In other words, the development of the oracy skills of speaking and auding follows and is built upon a pre-linguistic cognitive content and conceptualizing ability. Said plainly, the child must have something to think about before the need for a language ability for sharing thoughts can and needs to arise. It is important that it be understood that this early, pre-linguistic cognitive content, or *knowledge,* is what will form the foundation for the acquisition of new knowledge over the lifetime of the person. Thus Miller's concern for the child's acquisition of literacy skills to obtain survival knowledge must be traced back to the child's pre-linguistic acquisition of knowledge, and later to his acquisition of knowledge of and via the oral language (learning by being told; Carroll, 1968). We see, then, that knowledge itself is the primary "tool skill" for acquiring further knowledge—whether by oracy or by literacy skills.

A final aspect of the model is that it asserts that the literacy skills utilize the same conceptual base (cognitive content; conceptualizing ability; knowledge) as is used in auding and speaking, *and* utilize the same signs and rules for sequencing those signs as is used in the oral language skills for receiving and expressing conceptualizations. Notice that this is an assertion based upon the developmental sequence; i.e., the literacy skills are built upon existing oracy skills as the end of a developmental sequence. This does not mean that once literacy skills are acquired, they do not contribute anything new to knowledge or language capability; clearly they do. What is asserted is that when the literacy skills are initially acquired, they are essentially to be construed as a second way of utilizing the same language system the child uses in speaking and auding. Presumably this is what Jenkins and Liberman (1972) refer to as being able to use language by eye as well as it is used by ear.

Closing the Language-By-Ear-and-By-Eye "Gap"

A fundamental hypothesis derivable from the developmental model is that a child's ability to comprehend language by auding will surpass his ability to comprehend language by reading during the early years of school until the reading skills are acquired, at which time ability to comprehend language by auding and by reading should become equal.

Although this seems like a very basic relationship to be explored if one is interested in understanding the acquisition of ability to language by eye as well as by ear, it turns out that there is absolutely no research specifically designed to find out how well non-literates can comprehend language by ear, and how long they require to learn to comprehend language by eye as well as they do by ear. In other words, how long, typically, does it take to "crack the code?" Some have speculated that it takes about the first 3 grades (Chall, 1973); others (Smith, 1975:188) assert that learning to read may take, typically, only a few weeks (for fifteen-year-old adolescents)!

In the absence of well-designed studies that might reveal something of the closing of the "gap" between languaging by ear and by eye, Sticht et al. (1974) reviewed some 44 studies that measured how well subjects at different grade levels could comprehend messages presented in spoken vs. written form. Figure 2 summarizes this review and shows, for each grade level, the proportion of studies in which auding (A) was found superior to (A>R), equal to (A=R) or inferior to (A<R) reading (R). It should

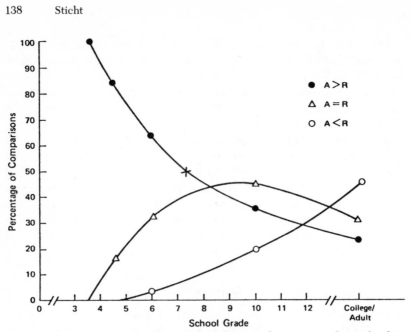

Figure 2. Comparison of auding and reading performance at five schooling levels.

be cautioned that these studies represent a wide variety of methods, messages, difficulty levels, response modes, etc.

   With these concerns in mind, the data of Figure 2 suggest that, clearly, children have not learned to comprehend by reading as well as they can comprehend by auding by the third grade. Learning to language by eye as well as one can language by ear may require as long as 7 school years or thereabouts, because it is at the seventh grade level where one has a fifty-fifty chance of finding studies showing auding ability greater than reading ability, and studies showing auding ability less than or equal to reading ability.

   Although, as mentioned, these data must be regarded with caution, there is some interesting additional circumstantial evidence that the learning-to-decode period may last as long as 7 or 8 years. One piece of evidence comes from the study of eye movement records, which indicate that it is not until the eighth grade that the adult pattern of eye movements during reading is typically achieved (Tinker, 1965:81–84). A second piece of evidence suggesting that learning to decode may take quite a while to fully develop comes from the work of Durrell and Brassard

(1969). These researchers developed a test to measure the "gap" between a person's ability to comprehend language by auding and by reading. The test includes four parts: vocabulary knowledge assessed via spoken and written modes, and comprehension of brief paragraphs presented in spoken and written forms. The data for a national norming sample ($N = 22,247$) indicate that auding and reading performance on the paragraph comprehension tests became equal during the sixth grade, while auding performance surpassed reading performance on the vocabulary knowledge subtests through the eighth grade. On the vocabulary and paragraph tests combined, auding and reading scores became equal in the eighth grade.

Comparisons of silent reading rates to typical auding rates provide additional evidence to suggest that it is around the seventh or eighth grade that the reading decoding process typically achieves the same degree of automaticity as is involved in auding. Data from the National Assessment of Educational Progress: Reading Rate (see Sticht et al., 1974:95) indicate that the silent reading rate for thirteen-year-olds (seventh and eighth graders) is around 175 wpm (words per minute). Earlier, Foulke and Sticht (1969) reported that the average oral reading rate of professional newscasters and readers for the blind is around 175 wpm. If this latter figure is regarded as a typical auding rate (because it is the rate professionals read aloud to be auded), then the silent reading rates of thirteen-year-olds closely matches the auding rates required when auding newscasts and similar formal spoken presentations. This might be construed as suggesting that reading and auding are operating with comparable degrees of automaticity of decoding at this age/grade level.

These various tenuous pieces of evidence suggest that one aspect of learning to read can indeed be considered as learning to language by eye as well as one can by ear. This is evidenced by the data that show that ability to comprehend by auding occurs first in the developmental sequence, and the person who acquires reading skill acquires the ability to comprehend by reading what he could earlier comprehend only by auding. Furthermore, this evidence suggests that, on the average, this aspect of learning to read may stretch from the first grade to the sixth, seventh, or eighth grades. Although it is not clear what exactly is occupying all this time, especially beyond the third or fourth grade, which reading specialists have traditionally considered the time frame for the "learning to read stage," it seems likely that this large time span is necessary for the child to develop full automatization of the reading decoding skill (LaBerge and Samuels, 1973).

If this analysis is correct, then perhaps learning to decode may be divided into two phases: in Phase One the child acquires the basic know-how of decoding, and in Phase Two the decoding skills are practiced and overlearned to the point of becoming completely automatic. This might correspond to the rapid growths and plateaus found in the development of many psychomotor skills. In this case, the rapid growth might correspond to the traditional "learning to read stage" during the first 3 years of schooling and the plateau would correspond to the development of full automaticity of deciding during the fourth to seventh or eighth years of schooling. (It should be noted that the data of Figure 2 suggest the possibility of even a third phase of learning to read, the stage in which some people appear to become more effective at getting information from texts than from spoken messages, as is the case for average high school seniors and collegians. This seems to represent a situation in which one is *better* able to language by eye than by ear, and may correspond to the phase in psychomoter skill development that occurs after the plateau phase. The NAEP data reported above suggest that most people do not acquire this post-plateau level of skill.)

STUDIES OF LEARNING
TO LANGUAGE BY EYE WITH ADULTS

In the foregoing discussion, learning to decode has been defined as that component of reading acquisition in which one becomes able to comprehend the written language as well as one can the spoken language. Learning to decode was further conceived as consisting of two phases. In Phase One, the early acquisition phase of learning to read, the person achieves the capability of decoding printed materials well enough to read and understand that which he can aud and understand—although the reading is not done with the same fluency with which auding is performed. In Phase Two, however, the reading decoding skills are practiced and overlearned to a level of automaticity comparable to that used in auding.

The studies to be described next are concerned with problems in measuring the Phase One and Phase Two skill levels with adult students of reading.

Measuring the "Gap" Between Auding and Reading Skills

In the course of our work to develop a reading program for adults (cf. Sticht, 1975; Sticht et al., 1975), we have been concerned with understanding various aspects of the "reading problem" the students exhibit. One thing we have considered is the extent to which their problem may be one of simply not being able to language by eye as well as they can by ear—the "reading problem" as defined by Jenkins and Liberman (1972).

To estimate the size of the "gap" between student's abilities to comprehend by auding and reading, we administered the Durrell Listening (called auding herein) and Reading Series Test: Intermediate Level to 116 male students in a literacy program in Northern California. Their ages ranged from 17 to 32 years, with a mean age of 19.5 years. School grades completed averaged 11.1, with a range from 7 to 16 (!). Over half had a high school diploma or equivalency certificate. Forty-five of the students spoke English as a second language, and were designated as the ESL group. Seventy-one spoke English as a primary language, and were designated the EPL group. (See Sticht and Beck, 1975, for a more complete description of this research, including results of additional testing of the auding-reading "gap," and a critique of tests for this purpose.)

The Durrell Listening and Reading Series (DLRS) Test provides three major pieces of information (all expressed in grade levels herein): a norm-referenced score on how well students can comprehend by auding; a norm-referenced score on how well they can comprehend by reading; and a derived score on what the reading level is that corresponds to the student's auding score (this latter information is called the reading "potential" score). Figure 3 presents a schematic model of the relationships of auding and reading over the early school years, and further explains the auding, reading, and reading potential scores.

Each of the three major pieces of information is divisible into two scores: one for vocabulary knowledge, and the other for paragraph comprehension. This information, along with the combined scores, is presented for the EPL and ESL groups separately in Table 1.

Looking first at Part C of Table 1, we can see that, even if these students learn to read as well as they can aud, they are going to have problems, because, although they are adults and most have high school or equivalency diplomas, their auding scores are at the fifth (EPL) and third (ESL) grade levels.

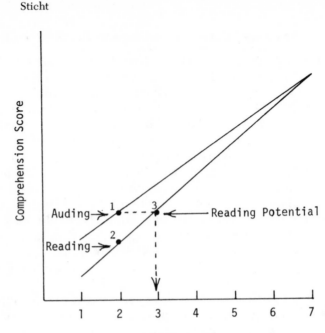

Figure 3. Schemata showing relationships among auding and reading comprehension scores as a function of school grade level. (Internal to the figure, #1 indicates the normative auding score for the second grade, called auding at the second grade level; #2 shows the normative reading score for the second grade, called reading at the second grade level; #3 shows conversion of the normative auding score to a reading "potential" score by drawing a horizontal from #1 to intersect with the reading curve, and then dropping a perpendicular line to the abscissa. The example shows a reading potential score of third grade. Thus the case illustrated shows a person auding and reading at the second grade level, with a reading potential score of third grade level.)

Part B of Table 1 presents reading grade level scores and Part A presents reading potential scores for EPL and ESL students. It is immediately apparent that these two groups differ considerably. For one thing, on the average, the EPL students are reading somewhat *below* their reading potential scores (5.8 to 4.9 = 0.9 grade levels, for total scores) while the ESL students appear to be reading *above* their reading potential level (4.1 to 4.8 = −0.7 grade levels, for total scores). This reflects the fact that the ESL students score very low on their ability to comprehend the spoken language (third grade level). No doubt we are detecting here what many of us have personally experienced in studying a foreign language: it is much easier to read the

Table 1. Grade equivalent group means and standard deviations on the Durell Listening and Reading Series Test

Test part and group	Vocabulary knowledge		Paragraph comprehension		Total	
	$\bar{\mathrm{X}}$	SD	$\bar{\mathrm{X}}$	SD	$\bar{\mathrm{X}}$	SD
Part A: Reading potential						
EPL[a]	6.02	1.18	5.46	1.61	5.77	1.17
ESL[b]	4.40	1.10	3.79	1.19	4.11	0.99
Total[c]	5.39	1.39	4.81	1.67	5.13	1.37
Part B: Reading						
EPL	4.87	1.36	5.08	1.59	4.92	1.32
ESL	4.84	1.29	4.75	1.48	4.76	1.23
Total	4.86	1.33	4.95	1.55	4.86	1.28
Part C: Auding						
EPL	5.27	1.42	5.17	2.10	5.21	1.40
ESL	3.20	1.48	3.04	1.50	3.03	1.49
Total	4.47	1.76	4.34	2.15	4.36	1.78

[a] Students speaking English as a primary language; $N = 71$.
[b] Students speaking English as a secondary language; $N = 45$.
[c] Total of both groups; $N = 116$.

language than it is to comprehend it in spoken form. Because most of the ESL students in this study had studied English in school, they developed more skill in reading than in auding the language.

Table 2 presents additional analyses emphasizing differences between results for the vocabulary and paragraph subtests for EPL and ESL students. Part A shows for the vocabulary subtests the number of students having reading potential (RP) scores greater than reading (R) scores (RP>R), reading scores greater than reading potential scores (R>RP), and equal reading potential and reading scores (RP=R). Here we see a complete reversal of the pattern for EPL and ESL students, with more than 80% of the EPL students showing RP>R, while over 75% of the ESL students show R>RP.

Part B of Table 2 shows for the paragraph subtests an enhanced effect for ESL students, with some 85% showing R>RP, while the EPL students show equal proportions having RP>R and R>RP. Though it is not certain what produced the differences between the vocabulary and paragraph subtests for EPL students, one possibility is that the memory load for the vocabulary subtest is more nearly equal in the auding and reading modes

Table 2. Cell frequencies comparing the number of testees whose reading potential is greater than their reading ability (RP > R), those whose reading ability is greater than their reading potential (R > RP), and those whose reading potential and ability are equal (RP = R)

Subtest and group	RP > R	R > RP	RP = R
Subtest A: Vocabulary knowledge			
EPL[a]	59	10	2
ESL[b]	10	33	2
Total[c] (N = 116)	69	43	4
Subtest B: Paragraph comprehension			
EPL	35	35	1
ESL	17	37	1
Total (N = 116)	42	72	2
Subtest totals			
EPL	53	13	5
ESL	4	36	5
Total (N = 116)	57	49	10

[a] Students speaking English as a primary language.
[b] Students speaking English as a secondary language.
[c] Total of both groups.

than it is in the paragraph subtests. In the Durrell Listening and Reading Series, the reading paragraphs are available throughout the response period, while the auding paragraphs are read aloud by the examiner and then the questions are asked. This places a much heavier load on memory during the auding paragraph test. This would then operate to *underestimate* the differences between comprehending by auding and reading.

Whatever the case, it seems from these data that many of the EPL students operate at such a low level of competence in the oral language that even if they learned to language by eye as well as they do by ear, they would still be some 5 to 6 grade levels below the average high school senior, and hence the "reading problem" in this case must be more broadly conceived to include a large "language problem."

Examining the Automaticity of Decoding Skills in Adult Literacy Students

As developed above, the second phase of learning to decode is the period during which the pupil develops *automaticity* of decoding. This means that the processing of print has become as automatic as the processing of speech, and is done in a completely unconscious manner, with the focus of attention on the conceptualizations being formed in accord with the printed message.

Because of the importance of acquiring automaticity, we have explored a method of evaluating a person's level of automaticity of decoding. Whereas it is possible to indirectly assess automaticity by measuring reading rate and comprehension, it is not clear in such instances whether a low reading rate implies poor decoding or difficulty of comprehension. If reading rate is high while comprehension is low, this may indicate that the reader skipped parts of the material. Because most procedures for measuring comprehension as a covariant of reading rate involve immediate retention tests of comprehension, it is not clear to what extent low comprehension may reflect a memory storage/retrieval problem rather than a decoding problem.

Ideally, what we would like is an "on-line" measure of decoding skill during silent reading, which could be coupled with an immediate retention test to serve as an indicator of information storage. However, this ideal is not attainable (at least we do not know how to attain it), hence an approximation to this ideal was sought. The procedure we finally developed consisted of presenting a simple story (fifth grade level, to be within the language level of the students) to be read while at the same time the story was presented in spoken form (on audiotape) to be auded. Then we arranged that at times during the presentation, there would occur a different, though semantically appropriate, word in the spoken message from what appeared on the printed page. For instance, the printed story might state "With the air of a *lord* he walked . . .," while the spoken story would state "With the air of a *prince* he walked . . ." When students encountered a mismatch, they were instructed to circle the printed word that did not match the spoken word. In order to perform this task, then, the students had to continually decode the print into a form comparable to the spoken word, and perform an internal comparison. To determine different levels of skill in performing this task, the audiotapes were time-compressed to produce speech rates of 228 and 328 wpm, while the uncompressed rate was 128 wpm.

To gain additional evidence that the "tracking" task described above (detecting mismatches between audio and printed words) does indeed involve continuous decoding, we prepared a second version of the same material, but in this case the mismatch word was replaced on the printed page by three words (see example), one of which matched the word in the spoken message. The student's task was then to circle the matching words.

Example: With the air of a king   he walked . . .
prince
lord

With such an arrangement, the student is able to skip a lot of the decoding required in the former task, because he has a cue as to where his next decision must be made. We refer to this version of the tracking task as the "cued" treatment, while the first version is called the "uncued" treatment.

The story used was a fifth grade version of Roland and Charlemagne. The first third of the story was presented at 128 wpm, the second third at 228 wpm, and the final third at 328 wpm. After each third of the selection, 15 four-alternative multiple choice questions were answered by the students. All questions called for retention of detail—no inference or reasoning items were included. These tests thus provided immediate retention indicators of comprehension.

Two groups of literacy program students were used. One group ($N=18$, mean reading grade level = 4.6 on the Metropolitan Intermediate Achievement Test: Reading) received the cued treatment, and a second group received the uncued treatment ($N=20$; reading grade level = 5.2).

Figure 4 presents the results of the two treatments: Part A presents the tracking data; Part B the immediate retention data. Of major interest is the difference between the curves for the cued and uncued tracking data (Part A). At the 128 wpm rate, the students in the uncued group scored only 60% correct on detection of mismatches. When the cues were added, this detection score increased to practically 100% correct. This adds credence to the notion that the tracking task does involve "on-line" decoding of print.

The fact that there is no difference to speak of between the immediate retention scores of the cued and uncued groups at the 128 wpm condition, may reflect a ceiling effect on the test (in fact, a group of college students scored only 85% correct on the test when administered following the same procedure as used in the present work). Why the cued group scored somewhat below the uncued group on the immediate retention tests is not clear

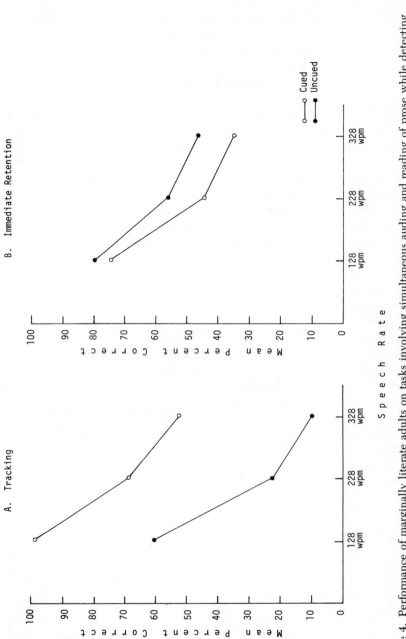

Figure 4. Performance of marginally literate adults on tasks involving simultaneous auding and reading of prose while detecting semantic mismatches (Part A) and recall of factual information (Part B).

(nor important to the present discussion), although it may reflect the fact that the mean reading level for the cued group was about 0.6 grade level below that of the uncued group.

The decline in the tracking and immediate retention scores for both the cued and uncued groups as the rate of speech was increased indicates that the ability of the students to both store information *and* perform the decoding task was impaired. This suggests that the use of accelerated speech rates can be used to apply stress to the students' information processing capabilities, and that ability to withstand this information processing overload, by keeping decoding and retention scores high, can indicate a higher level of skill in these capabilities.

Based on the above reasoning, the cued treatment was administered to a group of fifth grade students, reading at the fifth grade level; a group of young men in a literacy school, reading at the eighth grade level; and a group of out-of-school young men reading at the fourth grade level; and a group of college students reading above the eleventh grade level.

Figure 5 shows the data for these groups and the data for the cued treatment from Figure 4A. Part A shows the tracking (decoding) scores. Of interest here is that, although all groups were equally capable at the 128 wpm rate, differences among the groups appear at the faster rates. Surprisingly, the fifth grade students performed better than either of the literacy training groups, even though one of these groups read at the eighth grade level (as determined by the Metropolitan Achievement Test, Intermediate Level, 1968). The fifth graders also retained information (Part B) as well as the adult literacy students who read at the eighth grade level, and outperformed the adults reading at the fourth grade level. In both the tracking and immediate retention tasks, the college students excelled, with only trivial effects of rate to speak of.

The data of Figure 5, Part A (Tracking), indicate differences in the automaticity of decoding skills among these four groups. A point of major concern for those interested in adult reading training is that adults who score, on the average, at the eighth grade level on a standardized test may be less developed than a group of average (in terms of reading scores) fifth graders in automaticity of decoding. If, as suggested earlier, the development of automaticity ordinarily requires 3 to 5 years beyond the third grade for the "typical" child growing up in our kindergarten to twelfth

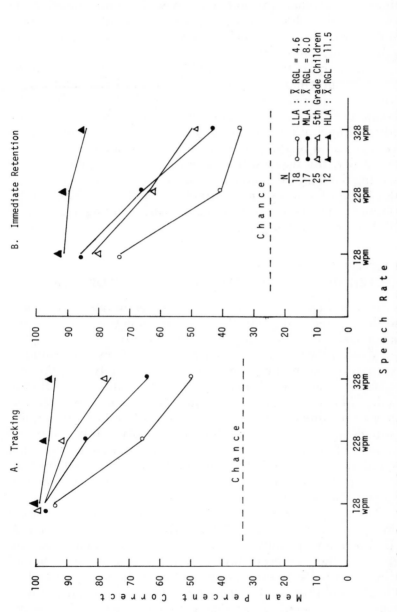

Figure 5. Results of tasks involving simultaneous auding and reading of prose while detecting semantic mismatches (Part A) and recall of factual information (Part B) for fifth grade children and adults of low (LLA), moderate (MLA), and high literacy ability (HLA) at the indicated mean reacting grade levels (RGL).

grade school curriculum, then we must consider that the development of comparable automaticity will require considerable time for adults who are learning to read. But adults in literacy training programs are typically interested in rapid acquisition of reading skills; and indeed numerous adult literacy programs exist that purport to "teach reading" very rapidly. And, as reported earlier, some researchers seem to think that adolescents might learn to read in ". . . a few weeks" (Smith, 1975:188). Perhaps the Phase One skills of learning to read may be acquired fairly rapidly, but full automaticity would seem to require extensive practice in reading over an extended period of time.

Clearly, the data presented here are only exploratory and anything but definitive; nonetheless they should cause us to consider further the problems, instructional and operational, of developing and assessing full automaticity of decoding in adult and childhood reading programs.

LEARNING TO USE THE
PRINTED MEDIUM FOR LITERACY TASK PERFORMANCE

As discussed above, one aspect of becoming literate is to learn to use the printed code with the same efficiency as one uses the spoken code in auding; i.e., to read efficiently.

A second aspect of achieving literacy involves learning to use the printed medium for performing a variety of tasks that demand a variety of information processing skills in addition to reading. Many of the tasks will require writing; most will require repeated reading of some materials; and still others will require reading while examining non-linguistic displays. It is in the performance of various tasks in which written materials are used that the unique properties of writing, and the printed media in general, seem to come to contribute most to the development of "literacy," as contrasted with "reading."

The unique aspects of written messages that set them apart from spoken messages are: 1) they are more or less permanent; and 2) they are spatially arrayed. Because written messages are permanent (i.e., not occurring "on-line" as in a live speech) and arranged spatially (both on a page and as a volume of pages when in book form) they can be *surveyed* so that readers can mobilize such content-related knowledge as they may have to relate the information in the text to what they know (i.e., to comprehend;

Smith, 1975). Because the text is more or less permanent, it is *referable;* i.e., the reader can flip back and forth to preview and review, and the text can be returned to at a later date for a rehearsal of what was previously read.

The reader may have recognized the foregoing as a paraphrase of Robinson's (1961) well-known reading study skills method, the SQ3R procedure. This procedure calls for first *surveying* a chapter (or other segment of writing), and noting headings, italicized words, topic sentences, etc., to form a general idea about what is in the material to be learned. Next the student *questions* himself about what is likely to be found in the reading; then the student *reads* the material, *recites* to himself the major points encountered and how they relate to the questions he formed; and finally, at a later date, the student *reviews* the chapter once again. Clearly, this procedure reflects the nature of texts as spatially arrayed and more or less permanent.

It is only because texts are pre-existing and permanent to a degree that the very complex literacy tasks like those referred to by Adler and Van Doren (1972) as *syntopical* reading can be performed. Such tasks involve the type of activities that are engaged in when preparing a "state-of-the-art" review; or when preparing a scholarly text, such as Huey's (1968) text on reading. Such tasks may take years to perform, and dozens of books may be skimmed, surveyed, noted, read, re-read, consulted, examined and dismissed, etc. This type of literacy activity requires much more than reading; it requires writing, editing, rewriting, discussions with people about the ideas being worked on, and much thinking!

At a considerably less grand level of performance, students may be called upon to write reports of what they have read; they may have to prepare a term paper for which they do considerable reading; they may have to prepare outlines, summaries, "300-word" abstracts, and the like about what they have read. In all of these cases, the reading materials are more than likely available during the production of the report. And it may be that only by attempting to prepare the report does the student become fully aware of the range of information in the materials being read. Thus in the course of writing, and after examining one's writing, the significance of what was previously read but discounted may be appreciated. In certain cases, the analysis and reasoning that may go into trying to write may transfer to reading, in which case the reader may detect previously unnoticed inconsistencies in what was earlier read, although to my knowledge we have no clear-cut evidence regarding the improvement of reading comprehension by writing (see Stotsky, 1975, for a review of literature in this area).

A particularly unique aspect of reading, as distinct from auding, arises from the fact that the printed word can be arrayed spatially. Thus we find figures and graphs with labeled axes and internal parameters, charts and tables, and illustrations with "call-outs" for identifying parts of the illustration. At times, comprehension of what is being read is contingent upon being able to comprehend the accompanying figure, table, etc. At other times, performance of some task, such as repairing a motor vehicle, may require the reading of language arrayed in a special "trouble-shooting" table. In such cases, if the structural properties of the table are not well understood, reading comprehension may be disrupted, especially if it is necessary to combine information from different parts of the table. Again, we may find that the use of a particular mode of representing thoughts may cause a change in a person's ability to comprehend what he reads. For instance, the use of row-by-column figures for sorting out treatments in analysis of variance designs may transfer to an almost habitual casting of problems that a person reads about into similar row-by-column representations in order to comprehend the various effects and their interactions being discussed. Again, however, no research along these lines is available.

Although there are certainly other tasks people perform with printed materials, the ones discussed above are sufficient to make the point that much of the acquisition of literacy is not simply learning to read, i.e., learning a substitute language system for the oral language system. Rather, a large part of learning to be literate, and perhaps the most important part for acquiring higher levels of literacy, is learning how to perform the many tasks made possible by the unique characteristics of printed displays, their permanence and spatiality. It may be that it is impossible to sort out the differential contributions to literacy of such activities as studying, writing, studying what one has written and revising it, and learning to use graphic information, tables, and various visual representations that combine writing with other visual data. But it is certainly the case that people must be able to perform all of these tasks involving reading if they are to be considered literate.

In the following section, a generalization is presented of the developmental model described earlier. This generalization incorporates the *production* of information displays, linguistic and non-linguistic, into the model, and represents an initial attempt to incorporate some of the literacy tasks described above into the developmental model of literacy.

GENERALIZING THE SIMPLE MODEL
OF THE DEVELOPMENT OF LITERACY
TO INCLUDE A BROADER RANGE OF LITERACY TASKS

Earlier, the simple model of the development of literacy skills shown in Figure 1 was described briefly. There it was pointed out that both speaking and writing are processes for representing thoughts in external displays, which people learn to decode to form internal representations (called conceptualizations) through the processes of auding and reading, respectively. Now it should be noted that there are other methods of representing conceptualizations externally than the linguistic modes. People can draw pictures, for instance, or produce gestures or bodily postures. Or we can externally represent thoughts through a combination of linguistic and non-linguistic representations: figures, graphs, tables; we can record our speech and gestures on videocassettes; and so forth.

To bring some order into all of these modes of representation of conceptualizations, they have been divided into three main categories: iconic, schematic, and linguistic modes of representation. Now it is assumed that by means of mental "programs" we have stored in our memories, we are able to externalize certain of our concepts by drawing pictures; it is this type of representation that, following Neisser (1967) and others before him, is referred to as *iconic* representation. *Linguistic* representation of conceptualizations is produced by speech or writing, and *schematic* representations are an admixture of iconic and linguistic representations—for example, flow charts, tables, graphs, etc.— that contain both visual structural features and (generally) linguistic signs in the forms of labels or short phrases.

These various representations are *displays* of information that can be examined by others; i.e., we can consider that there are three categories of *input display*—iconic, schematic, and linguistic—that people can attend to. Furthermore, the information in a given type of display—say a linguistic display—may, at

Figure 6. Example of iconic representation.

times, be representable in some other type of representation—
say an iconic representation. For example, information presented
in written form might be used as source material from which a
picture might be drawn that could represent essentially the same
meaning as in the written message. Thus, for instance, one may
write "The cave man threw a rock into the water." This might
alternatively be represented as Figure 6.

As another example, one might say "In our research project
we found that as the number of years of education increased, the
reading skill level increased up to about the tenth grade, and
remained the same thereafter." Alternatively, one might draw
Figure 7 and say that: "Figure 7 shows the results of our study.
Clearly reading skill is a function of years of education, at least
for up to 10 years of education."

As a final example, one might wish to explain to someone
that:

> You are eligible to apply for an old age pension if you are 65 years
> old and have contributed to the fund for at least five years. How-
> ever, if the five years of your contribution were prior to 1970, then
> you are not entitled to the full pension, but rather to ½ pension if
> you are 65, and ¾ if you are starting at age 67. . . ."

Alternatively, one could represent this as in Figure 8.

As indicated, then, it is possible to express very nearly the
same ideas in alternate modes: iconic, schematic, and linguistic.
Of course, there are conceptualizations that can only be represented in one or the other modes. And there are cases when
representation in one mode is better for some purpose than an
alternative mode.

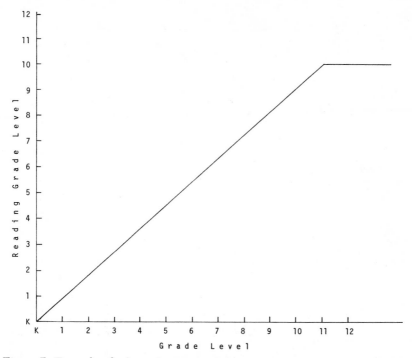

Figure 7. Example of schematic representation.

Using the Concept of
Alternative Modes of Representation in Literacy Training

Figure 9 schematizes the manner in which we have used the concept of alternative modes of representation in a literacy training program. We provide input representations in the form of two types of linguistic displays: spoken instructions and a written passage. The student is required to transform the written display into either an iconic display, by drawing a picture representing some portion of the written passage, or a schematic display, such as a flow chart or classification table with rows specifying concepts and columns listing attributes, or the like. Having made this linguistic-to-iconic or linguistic-to-schematic transformation, the student is then required to transform his product into a linguistic form again by orally describing what his product depicts.

There are several interesting features of this conceptual approach to literacy training that should be noted:

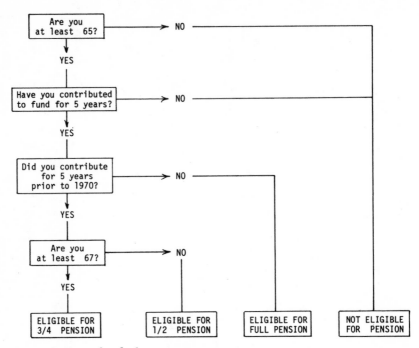

Figure 8. Example of schematic representation.

1. It encompasses the concept of reading as learning to language by eye as well as one can by ear by considering reading as linguistic-to-linguistic transformations of printed words into spoken words.

2. It includes the evaluation of comprehension by paraphrase, as Anderson (1972) recommends, by considering paraphrase as a type of linguistic-to-linguistic transformation.

3. It incorporates methods of indicating comprehension that de-emphasize memory, and that take advantage of the unique properties of printed displays—their permanence and spatiality—by permitting the source display to remain available while the student searches it to find needed information to transform and represent the information iconically or schematically (which are themselves modes of representation emphasizing the spatial display of information in ordered relationships, just as written prose does).

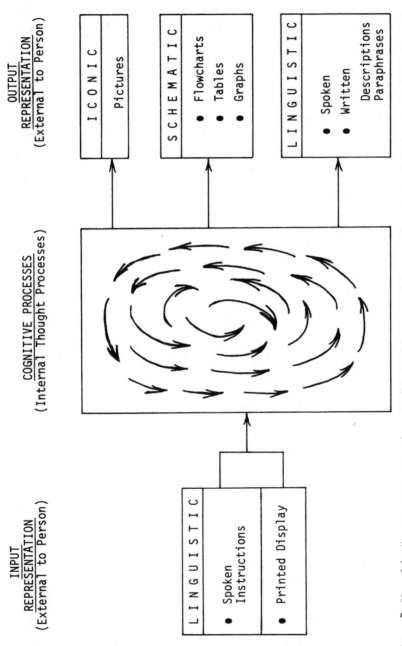

Figure 9. Use of the "representation transformation" (retran) literacy training procedure (printed displays in the form of narrative prose are transformed into an iconic, a schematic, or another linguistic representation of the information contained in the input display).

4.   It provides a framework for discussing literacy as a "key tool" for acquiring knowledge in a very pragmatic way by interpreting the roles of writers, editors, and illustrators as performing various transformations on input displays to create new output displays. For instance, writers study iconic, schematic, and linguistic displays and transform them into linguistic (written) output displays; editors take the output of the writer and perform linguistic-to-linguistic transformations, and illustrators take the writer's output and transform aspects of it into iconic output displays. Although this obviously simplifies matters somewhat, it nevertheless provides a pragmatic tie between reading and writing that may be of motivational value when dealing with career-oriented adults.

5.   There is a substantial research base becoming available that the "representation transformation" (retran) concept structures and subsumes at a highly superordinate level; for instance, Musgrave and Cohen (1971) discuss methods of transforming certain prose passages into two-way tables of information such that the underlying structure of the information contained in the passage may be perceived more readily and the relationships between its several parts can be considered one at a time. They further discuss the transformation of the two-way tables into lists of stimulus/response terms so that traditional verbal learning studies may be related to prose learning via the mediation of two-way tables. Although they emphasize the transformations for studying learning of textual materials, interest can be focused first directly on the transformational process itself and second on learning, which provides a more complete analysis of textual information processing relevant to the present concerns. Frase (1975), too, has studied prose that can be organized into two-way tables to study learning of textual material, and again we can adapt some of his approaches to study the transformation process itself. Lewis (1970) represents a line of research being pursued by several investigators on the representation of prose texts as logical trees, decision logic tables, and algorithmic flow-charts. This work provides formal principles for transforming narrative instructional texts into representations of the type illustrated in Figure 8. Macdonald-Ross and Smith (1974) pre-

sent an extensive bibliography on research concerned with the production of graphs, tables, figures, algorithms, readability (which relates nicely to the linguistic-to-linguistic transformation concept), and other research relevant to the types of transformations we are talking about here.

To date, our experience with the representation transformation concept has been limited to using it as a conceptual link between the development model of literacy outlined in Figure 1, in which we talk about the external representation of internal conceptualizations, and the development of·literacy training tasks that utilize the wide range of display types in which people must learn to be literate, in addition to narrative prose. We have found that by following the practice of showing an example, providing a demonstration, and then providing for guided practice, many of the young adults with whom we have worked can learn to perform the desired transformations. From future studies of teacher/student interactions, we hope to better understand the processes involved in executing the various transformations called for.

SUMMARY

What does it mean to achieve literacy, and what are the realistic possibilities for achieving literacy as an adult? Clearly these are questions of considerable import, and just as clearly, they have not been answered completely in this chapter. However, a dialogue has been opened so that the consideration of the acquisition of reading—the theme of this book—might be viewed in the larger context of the acquisition of literacy.

In response to the question of what it means to achieve literacy, it is suggested that there are at least two major, interdependent learning "strands." One is learning to language by eye as well as one can by ear; this is what is meant by learning to read. Furthermore, evidence is presented to suggest that this aspect of learning may involve two "stages": the learning of the knowledges and skills required to decode printed words into language, and the subsequent practice of this skill until automaticity is acquired.

The second major strand overlaps with the first and refers to learning the new vocabulary and concepts found in the printed materials one uses in learning to read, and includes the learning of new skills for processing information from printed displays based on the unique properties of such displays—their permanence and spatiality. In the section just preceding this one, a simple conceptual scheme is presented that we have found useful for developing instructional activities to teach some of the advanced literacy skills that result from applying reading to a variety of graphic displays.

In response to the question of what the realistic possibilities are for teaching adults to read, it is fair to say that data presented suggest that we need to have a much better understanding of the wide variety of adults who are learning to read, and we need to have a dialogue on the funds and effort we are willing, as a nation, to devote to better understanding the problems of adult illiterates or marginally literates. Most evidence suggests that most Adult Basic Education programs are able to "hold" students for only very limited amounts of training, say 100 to 200 hours, and may effect a one- or two-grade-level gain in reading skills, as measured by standardized tests (though most of the data may be suspect due to routine failure to consider regression effects). As evidenced herein, being able to read at the eighth grade level as an adult does not necessarily imply that one possesses the automaticity of reading of children who may be even three years below that reading level. Thus, it seems to me that strong attention needs to be given to providing *extensive* reading training for adults, so that automaticity of reading skills can be fully developed, and so that the advanced information processing skills involved in processing various graphic displays can be developed. The very brief efforts that currently abound do not produce sufficiently effective gains in literacy skills to permit them to function as "key tools" for the acquisition of knowledge of the type and in the amount needed to successfully pursue "the good life" beyond the "level of existence we call welfare."

REFERENCES

Adler, M., and Van Doren, C. 1972. How to Read a Book. New York: Simon and Schuster.

Anderson, R. C. 1972. How to construct achievement tests to assess comprehension. Review of Educational Research 42:145–170.

Carroll, J. B. 1968. On learning from being told. Educational Psychologist 5:5–10.

Chall, J. S. 1973. Learning to read. In G. Miller (ed.), Communication, Language, and Meaning. New York: Basic Books.

Durrell, D., and Brassard, M. 1969. Listening Reading Series. New York: Harcourt, Brace, & World.

Foulke, E., and Sticht, T. 1969. A review of research on the intelligibility and comprehension of accelerated speech. Psychological Bulletin 72:50–62.

Frase, L. T. 1975. Advances in research and theory in instructional technology. In F. N. Kerlinger (ed.), Review of Research in Education. Itaska, Ill.: F. E. Peacock Pubs., Inc.

Huey, E. B. 1968. The Psychology and Pedagogy of Reading. (Originally published in 1908 by Macmillan.) Cambridge, Mass.: M.I.T. Press.

Jenkins, J., and Liberman, A. 1972. Background to the conference. In J. F. Kavanagh and I. G. Mattingly (eds.), Language by Ear and by Eye. Cambridge, Mass.: M.I.T. Press.

Kavanagh, J. F., and Mattingly, I. G. (eds.) 1972. Language by Ear and by Eye. Cambridge, Mass.: M.I.T. Press.

LaBerge, D., and Samuels, S. J. 1973. Toward a Theory of Automatic Information Processing in Reading. Report No. 3, Minnesota Reading Research Project. Minneapolis: University of Minnesota Press.

Lewis, B. N. 1970. Decision logic tables for algorithms and logical trees. CAS Occasional Paper number 12. London: Her Majesty's Stationery Office.

Macdonald-Ross, M., and Smith, E. B. 1974. Bibliography for Textual Communication. Monograph No. 3. Milton Keynes, England: Institute of Educational Technology, The Open University.

Miller, G. A. 1972. Reflections on the conference. In J. F. Kavanagh and I. G. Mattingly (eds.), Language by Ear and by Eye. Cambridge, Mass.: M.I.T. Press.

Murphy, R. T. 1975. Assessment of adult reading competence. In D. Nielsen and H. Hjelm (eds.), Reading and Career Education. Newark, De.: International Reading Association.

Musgrave, B., and Cohen, J. 1971. Relationships between prose and list learning. In E. Rothkopf and P. Johnson (eds.), Verbal Learning Research and the Technology of Written Instruction. New York: Teachers College Press.

National Assessment of Educational Progress. 1972. Report 02-R-00: Reading: Summary. Education Commission of the States, May, Denver, Colo.

Neisser, U. 1967. Cognitive Psychology. New York: Appleton-Century-Crofts.

Northcutt, N. 1975. Functional literacy for adults. In D. Nielsen and H. Hjelm (eds.), Reading and Career Education. Newark, De.: International Reading Association.

Robinson, F. P. 1961. Effective Study. New York: Harper and Row.

Smith, F. 1975. Comprehension and Learning. Toronto: Holt, Rinehart and Winston.

Sticht, T. G. (ed.) 1975. Reading for Working. Alexandria, Va.: Human Resources Research Organization.

Sticht, T. G. et al. 1975. A Program of Army Functional Job Reading Training: Development, Implementation, and Delivery Systems.

Draft Technical Report. Alexandria, Va.: Human Resources Research Organization.

Sticht, T. G., and Beck, L. 1975. Assessing Differences in Auding and Reading Skills of Adults. Draft Interim Report. Alexandria, Va.: Human Resources Research Organization.

Sticht, T. G., Beck, L., Hauke, R., Kleiman, G., and James, J. 1974. Auding and Reading: A Developmental Model. Alexandria, Va.: Human Resources Research Organization.

Stotsky, S. L. 1975. Sentence-combining as a curricular activity: its effect on written language development and reading comprehension. Research in the Teaching of English 9:30–71.

Tinker, M. A. 1965. Bases for Effective Reading. Minneapolis: University of Minnesota Press.

A RESPONSE:
Comments on Language by Eye and by Ear

Ludwig Mosberg

Dr. Sticht has performed a great service by reminding us that reading acquisition is not a problem restricted to childhood. Although it is, of course, true that the problem of the adult nonreader would not exist if the problem of reading acquisition for children had been solved, nevertheless, as Sticht points out, there are literally millions of American adults who are functional nonreaders. This obviously represents a great national problem that, unfortunately, has not received the attention it deserves by those concerned with reading acquisition. It is encouraging, however, that adult nonreading has recently been recognized as a problem by a number of federal and state agencies that have stimulated considerable interest in this issue among psychologists and educators like Sticht. Although the problem is no less severe, it is fair to say that we know even less about reading acquisition by adults than we do about reading acquisition by children.

Sticht makes a useful distinction between "reading" and "literacy." As to the "reading problem," the Jenkins and Lieberman (1972) remark that "at all events the reading problem as we know it would not exist, if in dealing with language all children could do as well by eye as they do by ear" has much to recommend it. This conception delimits what is meant by the rubric "reading" to a manageable yet nontrivial definition. One of the most serious problems in reading research and in teaching reading is that there is a tendency to include virtually all psychological processes in our definition of reading, with the result that we lose sight of the real problem. The fact that a child or an adult who does not do well by ear will, most likely, also not do well in reading, is not a "reading problem" but rather is a "language problem." This language problem cannot be solved by studying reading acquisition, but the reading problem could be solved by identifying and teaching those skills necessary for the individual to use written language at least at the same extent as oral language is used by the individual. Increasing the child's or adult's knowledge of the language transcends the particular mode of representation, i.e., speaking or writing, listening or reading. Until the critical distinction between reading and languaging is recognized and accepted, the "reading problem" will be forever with us.

This line of argument suggests, particularly in conjunction with Sticht's remarks concerning closing the "gap" between language by ear and language by eye, that the study of reading acquisition and performance be concerned with the direction and size of this "gap." It suggests that poor readers be redefined as those whose auding is significantly better than their reading; that good readers are those for whom the "gap" is not significantly different from zero; and that excellent readers are those whose reading is significantly better than their auding. These measurement definitions separate language ability from reading ability.

In his model Sticht asserts that both oral language and written language utilize the same signs and rules for sequencing those signs in receiving and expressing conceptualizations. For most children and adults this assertion is probably true. However, for a sizable proportion of children and for a sizable proportion of those 18 million adults who cannot properly fill out their Social Security forms, the assertion is probably false. It may be precisely because this assertion is false that so many children and adults have difficulty learning to read. This assertion in Sticht's model does not take into account the systematic variations in syntax, semantics, and phonology present in our society, amply demonstrated by Labov (1972), for example, in his studies of Black English dialect, or by other numerous children and adults for whom English is a second language. Although there is considerable controversy regarding the influence of dialect on reading (see Gibson and Levin, 1975; Sommervill, 1975; Harber and Bryen, 1976), the possible direct negative effects or the more indirect motivational effects of non-standard English speech on learning to read at the elementary level cannot be ruled out. It is precisely these populations in which the "reading problem" tends to be most manifest.

It is possible that for many children and adults the existing oracy skills are simply inappropriate to written language; hence the reading problem. Most of what children and adults read is written in Standard English (SE). While SE has more in common with non-SE dialects than it has differences, the differences may nevertheless present serious reading problems to a non-SE speaker. For example, Hall et al. (1977) have shown that even for orally presented stories, young black urban children recalled short stories reliably better when presented in Black Vernacular English than when presented in SE. Their recall of stories presented to them in SE was significantly lower than SE-speaking urban white children's recall. Of particular interest, however, is the fact that both black and white groups performed equally well when the stories were presented to them in their own dialect. Thus, one must question Sticht's statement that "when literacy skills are initially acquired, they are essentially to be construed as a second way of utilizing the same language system the child uses in speaking and auding" (this volume). All one has to do is to listen to black ghetto children, for example, speak among themselves and compare this speech with written material in the classroom to be convinced that the two do not represent the *same* language system.

This may even be true of so-called SE-speaking children when compared to SE-speaking adults. Children and adults do not use identical language systems. An examination of reading primers (Hatch, 1969) that are written by adults clearly demonstrates that primers often contain syntactic constructions that children do not comprehend. Yet when the child is given a reading comprehension test and does poorly, we call him a poor reader, when in fact it has little to do with reading but perhaps a great deal to do with the lack of congruence between the language of the adult author and the language of the child. What may happen all too often is that for children whose language is sufficiently different from the language of instruction, learning to read is extremely frustrating, which leads the child to simply give up. These children may become our adult nonreaders, some of whom, for one reason or another, get motivated again to learn to read, enroll in adult reading courses, find the same frustrations, and give up again. Perhaps this is why, as Sticht points out, Adult Basic Education courses cannot hold on to these adult students for very long. It is likely that if schooling were not compulsory we could not hold on to them as children either. We may be forced to face the possibility that in order to teach these children and adults to read we must first teach them a language of instruction. The alternative may be to teach reading in the language the learner brings to the task. Sommervill (1975) has pointed out that neither of these nor other alternatives have been adequately investigated. However, if we are really serious about the "reading problem" for those most affected, this issue will eventually have to be met head on.

In conclusion, some qualifications on the experiments Sticht reported on automaticity of decoding skills are warranted. Recall that subjects were given a tracking task in which they had to determine mismatches between what was said and what was written. There was both a cued and a non-cued condition and all groups received an immediate retention test. In the first part of the study, Sticht compared the cued and non-cued conditions with subjects who read at the fifth grade level. On the tracking task, under all speech rates, the cued condition led to superior performance compared to the uncued condition. However, on the immediate retention test there was no difference between the cued and non-cued conditions at the 128 wpm rate although there were significant differences at the 228 and 328 wpm rates (cued condition lower than uncued condition). Sticht argued that across all speech rates the cued groups scored below the uncued groups on the immediate retention test because the mean reading levels of the cued group was about 0.6 of a grade level below the mean of the uncued group. A different explanation may be more plausible. As Sticht pointed out in the description of the study, the cued condition task does not require the subject to attend to all parts of the passage equally; he need only attend to the cued words. The subjects in the uncued condition must attend to the entire passage and they do better on the retention test perhaps because more of the passage has been actively processed by them. The fact that at the slower 128 wpm rate there was no difference on the retention test may reflect, as Sticht suggested, nothing more than a ceiling effect.

Sticht argued that the differences in the tracking task among his four groups in the second part of the experiment reflected differences in automaticity of decoding. In what sense do these data from the tracking task say anything about automaticity of decoding skills? According to LaBerge and Samuels (1974) the "criteria for decoding when a skill or subskill is automatic is that it can complete its processing while attention is directed elsewhere." In Sticht's experiment it is not clear to what the subject was directing his attention, nor is it clear what the relationship was between correct recognition of mismatches and automatic processing. In the LaBerge and Samuels model, attention is assumed to be necessary for accuracy of response but attention by definition is not necessary for automaticity. Therefore, it is not clear that accuracy in Sticht's tracking task is even a measure of automaticity, at least as LaBerge and Samuels have defined it. What Sticht may have measured here is tracking ability rather than decoding automaticity. It is possible that Sticht might find the same results no matter what the stimuli were in this task. In that case it is unlikely that the results would be interpreted as automaticity of decoding skills but rather would be interpreted as an indication simply of differences in general tracking ability.

REFERENCES

Gibson, E. J., and Levin, H. 1975. The Psychology of Reading. Cambridge, Mass.: M.I.T. Press.

Hall, W. S., Cole, M., and Reder, S. 1977. Variations in young children's use of language. In R. O. Freedle (ed.), Discourse Production and Comprehension. Norwood, N.J.: Ablex Publishing Co.

Harber, J. R., and Bryen, D. N. 1976. Black English and the reading task. Review of Educational Research 46:387–405.

Hatch, E. 1969. The Syntax of Four Reading Programs Compared with Language Development of Children. Technical Report No. 22. Los Alamitos, Ca. Southwest Regional Laboratory.

Jenkins, J. J., and Liberman, A. M. 1972. Background to the conference. In J. F. Kavanagh and I. G. Mattingly (eds.), Language by Ear and by Eye. Cambridge, Mass.: M.I.T. Press.

LaBerge, D., and Samuels, S. J. 1974. Toward a theory of automatic information processing in reading. Cognitive Psychology 2:293–323.

Labov, W. 1972. Language in the Inner City. Philadelphia: University of Pennsylvania Press.

Somervill, M. A. 1975. Dialect and reading: A review of alternative solutions. Review of Educational Research 45:247–263.

Index

DATE DUE

DEMCO 38-297